Smart Selling℠ Techniques for New Home Salespeople

Volume 1: The Sequence for Success

A Complete Guide for Each Segment of an Effective

New Home Sales Presentation

Bob Schultz, MIRM, CSP
New Home Specialist℠ Inc.

North America's Foremost New Home
Sales & Management Expert

Smart Selling^{SM} Techniques for New Home Salespeople

Volume 1: The Sequence for Success

A Complete Guide for Each Segment of an Effective New Home Sales Presentation

What Words to Use, When to Use Them,

and How to Use Them

Legalities

Service and trademarks

The following services and products appear in these materials and are service/trademarks of New Home Specialist Inc.

New Home Specialist[SM]

The Five-Minute Professional[SM]

Situational Selling Techniques[SM]

Smart Selling[SM] Techniques

C.O.M.M.A.[SM]

The Sequence for Success[SM]

Selling 2000[SM]

Smart Start[SM]

Five-Minute Drill[SM]

Situational Selling[SM]

SST[SM]

Home Site Matrix[SM]

Slight Edge[SM]

Six Step Method[SM]

Managing 2000[SM]

New Home Specialist[SM] Education Systems

New Home Specialist[SM] Publishing Group

The Official New Home Sales Development System®

A registered trademark of New Home Specialist Inc.

"It Ain't Over… 'Til It's Over"[SM] and Follow-Through®

are registered service and trademarks of Hoffacker & Associates.

Realtor® is a registered collective membership mark that identifies a real estate professional who is a member of the National Association of REALTORS®.

Acknowledgments

Author

Bob Schultz, MIRM, CSP
    President, New Home Specialist Inc.

Editor and Contributor

Marilyn McVay, MIRM, CSP
    Vice President of Training and Development
    New Home Specialist Inc.

Contributor

Simon Crossley

Publication Coordinator

Peggy Burkett
    New Home Specialist Inc.

Production Manager

Donna Santoro
    New Home Specialist Inc.

Information Design

Cristine F. Fernández, MEd
    Red Sled Productions, LLC

Publication Editor

Jenifer F. Walker
    Cartref Communications

Cover Design

Group Two Advertising
    Philadelphia, PA

Publisher

New Home Specialist Publishing Group

About the Author

Experienced

With more than three decades of practical experience and success in the real estate and home building industries, Bob Schultz is widely recognized today as North America's foremost new home sales and management expert. Bob, along with licensed facilitators, conducts more than 250 custom sales and management training seminars and workshops each year to thousands of industry professionals throughout North America and around the world through in-company presentations and live video conferences. He is the Founder and President of New Home Specialist Inc., a full service training and sales management resource firm headquartered in Boca Raton, Florida. The company produces books, management systems, and video and audiocassette programs.

Award-Winning

Bob has received numerous awards for sales and marketing excellence, including special recognition as NAHB's Marketing Director of the Year, Large Volume. Dedicated to his profession, Bob is a Board member of the Institute of Residential Marketing (MIRM) and past vice president of the National Sales and Marketing Council (NSMC). He is a member of The National Speakers Association and has received its coveted Certified Speaking Professional designation. Bob is the author of *The Official Handbook for New Home Salespeople*, the most widely read and used book ever on new home sales, and the creator of *The Official New Home Sales Development System®*, a comprehensive video training program.

Contents

The Sequence for Success^{SM}

Overview

Professional selling is both an art (personality) and a process (system). To practice the art effectively, you must first master the process.

Observation

Failure that results from a well-conceived process that's implemented will be far more valuable than *success* in the absence of a process.

—Nido Qubein

What is a process?

A process is a series of events or stages of activity that takes place over time with continuity and has an identifiable purpose and result. A process can be replicated at will, and, more importantly, you can learn from mistakes if you fail when using a process. Success in the absence of a process may be nothing more than blind luck. Bob Schultz has formalized the new home sales process and distilled its essence in this book. The process you will follow is called the *Sequence for Success.*

The Sequence for Success

This book is designed to reinforce the importance of having a process. It gives specific strategies and scripts to use at different points in the process. The *Sequence for Success* consists of six phases.

▶ Preparation
▶ Presentation
▶ Demonstration/Selection
▶ Close
▶ Follow Up
▶ Customer Care

continued on the next page

The Sequence for Success *(Continued)*

PDR

As taught by legendary sales trainer, Tom Hopkins, using the Practice-Drill-Rehearse (PDR) method results in your mastery of a professional selling process that makes you unconsciously competent to perform under any circumstances. Competence leads to confidence. Confidence leads to increased opportunities.

Defining moments

Selling is like theatre. Each step in the professional sales process, like a scene in a play, has a defining moment that leads to the next step. These defining moments indicate to you that the customer is moving willingly in the right direction. The preparation, presentation, and demonstration steps lead you to the opportunity to close. By being proactive, you will create the defining moments.

The Sequence for Success

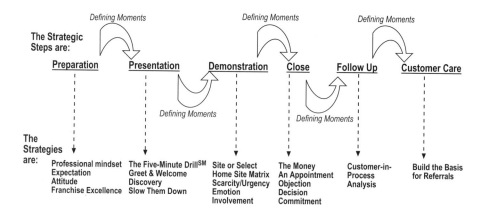

continued on the next page

The Sequence for Success *(Continued)*

About this book

This is a comprehensive resource that provides "the words to use"—from greeting through discovery to demonstration, and specific techniques for effective closing —to produce the defining moments you want. It provides all the "critical tools" you need to implement the *Sequence for Success.*

Many of the techniques presented in this book are "no calorie" techniques. If they don't work, you've lost nothing. If you do get a response, however, you can then move forward in a positive direction. This practical guide will soon become your working toolbox. It will serve and assist you during your daily quest for new home sales success.

Smart Selling Techniques

When used to their full potential, these Smart Selling Techniques (SST) will become an indispensable toolbox of effective, proven communication techniques.

A **situational scenario** sets the possible stage for using each technique. The corresponding **strategy** focuses you on the desired and expected outcome. Your success will be the result of concentrated thought—directed toward the situation—using knowledge, skill, and experience.

Customer's Comments

Words representing the prospective buyers' likely comments should not be construed as the only possible dialogue. The words are meant to anticipate likely conversations. For simplicity, the term customers always appears in the plural.

continued on the next page

The Sequence for Success *(Continued)*

Professional Communicator

Tremendous care has been given to provide practical and functional verbal guidelines for the professional communicator's dialogue. Each technique is designed to render the desired outcome and is the written version of countless hours of real-life performance and hands-on experience. In cases where you have a choice of wording based on your specific situation, you will see an "**(or)**" in the box.

Within the scripts, instructions appear to help you craft the pace, tone, and direction of the dialogue. When properly practiced and rehearsed, these Smart Selling Techniques will become natural, conversational, and convincing. Mastering them will require an investment of your time and a significant commitment from you.

Instructions — Instructions to you are shown in gray boxes. These are not part of dialogue but rather helpful hints and strategies.

Flowcharts

Each SST is presented in a flowchart format. This diagram-based chart represents the flow of the conversation between the professional communicator and the customers. By starting at the top and moving down along the vertical and horizontal lines, you can envision how the dialogue* develops. When a conversation could take alternative paths, the lines branch to the left and the right, indicating possible variations. Follow one branch at a time to get a sense of the continuity of the suggested conversation.

*Dialogue is a planned and practiced event. Your challenge is to make the dialogue you learn in this guide *feel* like a conversation.

continued on the next page

The Sequence for Success *(Continued)*

On the job

This book is designed to travel with you. Always by and on your side, this guidebook will accompany you at the sales office, in the model home, on a home site, in your car, walking through a field home, out on a job site, around the kitchen table, and at the closing table. It can go anywhere and everywhere.

The challenge to prepare

As the legendary coach, Vince Lombardi, said, "The will to win is important, but the will to prepare to win is vital." That principle is very important to your success with this dynamic guide. Each of these Smart Selling Techniques should be thoroughly read, examined, and re-read. An effective method for learning the vital concepts of each technique is to write them out for yourself (with only slight modification, if necessary, to make the script natural in tone, specific to your particular situation, and consistent with your speaking style).

A second recommendation is to read each script aloud, in front of a mirror, then progressing to an audio cassette, and if possible, to a video tape recording. Ultimately, the practice and rehearsal continues, using Simulated Selling scenarios with fellow salespeople and sales managers mentoring an interactive role-modeling format. Remember, the difference between *rehearsal* and *performance* is *practice* and *experience*.

continued on the next page

The Sequence for Success *(Continued)*

Good advice

As a professional communicator, you cannot allow your message to be misconstrued or misunderstood. Don't use industry slang with a prospective home buyer. It could create an ambiguous situation for the prospect. The customer may be confused and not understand what you intend. Say what you mean clearly and concisely.

When people don't communicate clearly, the listener might not understand the intended message. This semantic interference might create an incongruency with the speaker's objective. No one is sure what was said or what was heard.

Avoid such commonly used slang phrases that could cause ambiguity for your customers.

- Is this your first time?
- What's your time frame?
- What brings you out here today?
- Do you want to tie it up?
- Wanna take it off the market?
- So, whaddaya think?
- Let's wrap it up!

At all times refrain from using casual, slang phrases such as "you guys" when addressing customers.

Greeting/Welcome

Observation

You can have everything in life you want if you help enough other people get what they want.

-Zig Ziglar

Introduction

On the following pages you will find a specific situation, strategy, and rationale explained. The facing page shows the corresponding Smart Selling Technique.

Actual situations may vary slightly. You must apply your common sense and logic to use these techniques to their best advantage.

In this section

The following Smart Selling Techniques (SST) are crafted for use during the Greeting/Welcome phase of the *Sequence for Success*.

Greeting/Welcome *(Continued)*

GW1. Customers first enter your sales arena

Situation

Customers first enter your sales arena.

Strategy

Welcome the customers, give them your name, obtain and use their names, and establish how much time they have available so that you can control the process, using good people and communication skills.

Rationale

If you start out without knowing how much time the customer has to spend, you are starting in a vacuum. Although, you will often find that you'll get more time than the customers say they have. For example, when customers say they have 15 minutes, they will give you 25 minutes.

GW1. Customers first enter your sales arena.

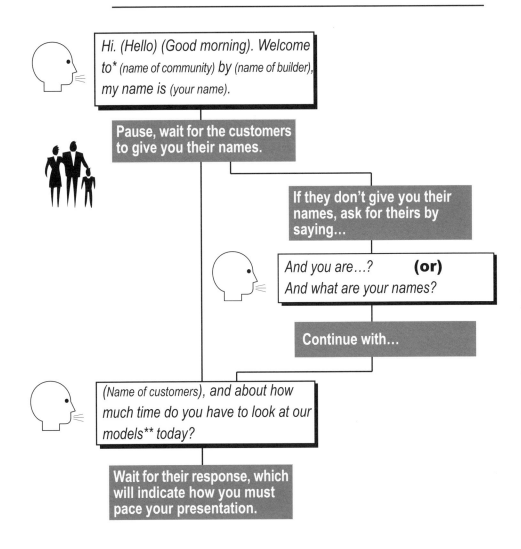

Hi. (Hello) (Good morning). Welcome to* (name of community) *by* (name of builder), *my name is* (your name).

Pause, wait for the customers to give you their names.

If they don't give you their names, ask for theirs by saying...

And you are...? **(or)**
And what are your names?

Continue with...

(Name of customers), *and about how much time do you have to look at our models** today?*

Wait for their response, which will indicate how you must pace your presentation.

*If your builder is the only entity in the neighborhood, state the name of the community first. If there are several builders in the community, state the name of the builder first. For example, "Welcome to ABC Builders at Crosscreek Estates."

**(or) homes (or) community (or) home sites, as the case may be.

Key

Customer response

Professional Communicator

Greeting/Welcome *(Continued)*

GW2. Customers in a hurry

Situation

Upon entering your sales arena, the customers indicate that they are in a hurry.

Strategy

Get the customers to commit to a specific amount of time and cause them to slow down.

Rationale

Always control the process, using good people and communication skills.

GW2. Upon entering your sales arena, the customers indicate that they are in a hurry.

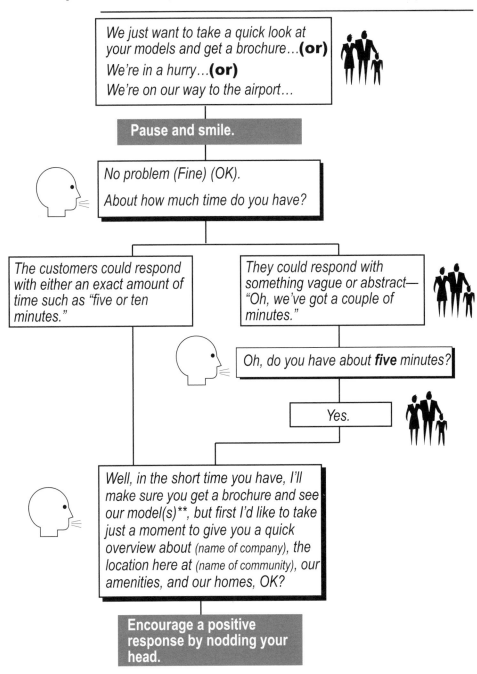

We just want to take a quick look at your models and get a brochure...**(or)**

We're in a hurry...**(or)**

We're on our way to the airport...

Pause and smile.

No problem (Fine) (OK).

About how much time do you have?

The customers could respond with either an exact amount of time such as "five or ten minutes."

They could respond with something vague or abstract— "Oh, we've got a couple of minutes."

Oh, do you have about **five** minutes?

Yes.

Well, in the short time you have, I'll make sure you get a brochure and see our model(s)**, but first I'd like to take just a moment to give you a quick overview about (name of company), the location here at (name of community), our amenities, and our homes, OK?

Encourage a positive response by nodding your head.

Key
Customer response
Professional Communicator

*(or) homes (or) community (or) home sites, as the case may be.

Greeting/Welcome *(Continued)*

GW3. There are more customers than you

Situation

There are more customers than you. For example, you encounter more than one prospective customer group to greet.

Strategy

Greet all of the individuals using a "group" greeting.

Rationale

Try to discern who amongst the prospective buyers might be the most interested.

GW3. There are more customers than you. For example, you encounter more than one prospective customer group to greet.

Hi (Hello) (Good morning/afternoon). Welcome to* (name of community) by (name of builder). My name is (your name). As you can see, we are very busy today. By the way, who is interested in getting some information about possibly owning a brand new home?

Then, shut up. Wait for customers to respond. Sometimes customers will raise their hands or point to each other. This response will single out the most likely prospects.

*If your builder is the only entity in the neighborhood, state the name of the community first. If there are several builders in the community, state the name of the builder first. For example, "Welcome to ABC Builders at Crosscreek Estates."

Key

Customer response

Professional Communicator

Greeting/Welcome *(Continued)*

GW4. The escape artist

Situation

The customer tries to brush you aside, ignore you, or "escape" into the model home.

Strategy

Maintain control of the presentation and slow the customer down.

Rationale

Many customers do not at first appreciate the type of information you can provide while in your sales arena or how it can really be very helpful to them.

GW4. The customer tries to brush you aside, ignore you, or "escape" into the model home.

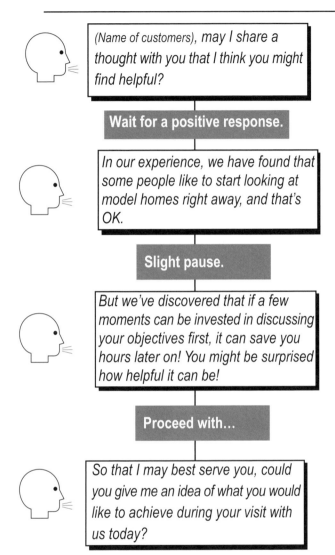

(Name of customers), may I share a thought with you that I think you might find helpful?

Wait for a positive response.

In our experience, we have found that some people like to start looking at model homes right away, and that's OK.

Slight pause.

But we've discovered that if a few moments can be invested in discussing your objectives first, it can save you hours later on! You might be surprised how helpful it can be!

Proceed with...

So that I may best serve you, could you give me an idea of what you would like to achieve during your visit with us today?

Key

Customer response

Professional Communicator

Greeting/Welcome *(Continued)*

GW5. The reluctant customer

Situation

After you have greeted the customers, they are reluctant to offer information or get involved with the dialogue attempts you are making.

Strategy

Reassure nervous customers that you and your company can be trusted.

Rationale

One of the six hidden fears of most home buying customers is doing business with a builder. You can proactively address that fear during the initial greeting and welcoming stage.

GW5. After you have greeted the customers, they are reluctant to offer information or get involved with the dialogue attempts you are making.

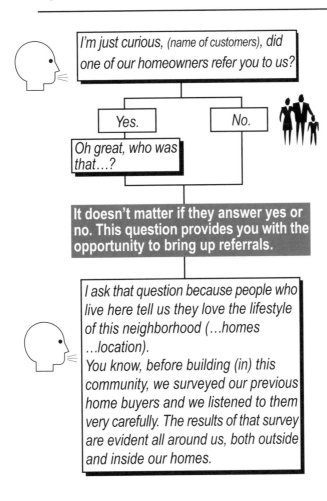

> I'm just curious, *(name of customers)*, did one of our homeowners refer you to us?

Yes. | No.

Oh great, who was that...?

It doesn't matter if they answer yes or no. This question provides you with the opportunity to bring up referrals.

> I ask that question because people who live here tell us they love the lifestyle of this neighborhood (...homes ...location).
> You know, before building (in) this community, we surveyed our previous home buyers and we listened to them very carefully. The results of that survey are evident all around us, both outside and inside our homes.

Key
Customer response — Professional Communicator

Greeting/Welcome *(Continued)*

GW6. Immediately looking for the deal

Situation

A customer asks—perhaps even before seeing the models—what incentives, deals, or "best" interest rates your community is offering.

Strategy

Have the customers sort through their priorities and "shelve" the discussion of deals and incentives until *after* they have experienced what you have to offer.

Rationale

Incentives, lowest price, or interest rates alone do not necessarily mean the best value.

GW6. A customer asks—perhaps even before seeing the models—what incentives, deals, or "best" interest rates your community is offering.

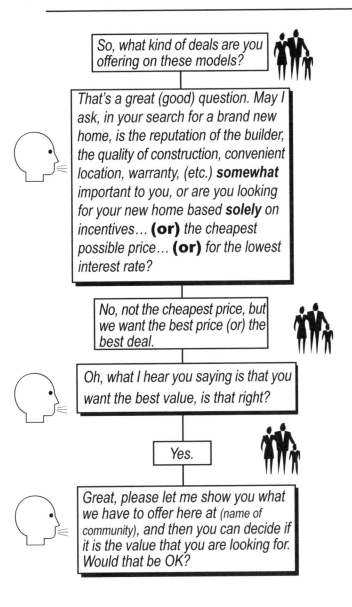

So, what kind of deals are you offering on these models?

That's a great (good) question. May I ask, in your search for a brand new home, is the reputation of the builder, the quality of construction, convenient location, warranty, (etc.) **somewhat** important to you, or are you looking for your new home based **solely** on incentives... **(or)** the cheapest possible price... **(or)** for the lowest interest rate?

No, not the cheapest price, but we want the best price (or) the best deal.

Oh, what I hear you saying is that you want the best value, is that right?

Yes.

Great, please let me show you what we have to offer here at (name of community), and then you can decide if it is the value that you are looking for. Would that be OK?

Key

Customer response

Professional Communicator

Greeting/Welcome *(Continued)*

GW7. Real estate agency disclosure requirement

Situation

States where real estate agency disclosure is required and applicable to your situation.

Strategy

Ask the customers if they are familiar with the disclosure form and present it to them.

Rationale

Completely and absolutely comply with the requirements of the law without becoming overly encumbered in the process.

GW7. States where real estate agency disclosure is required and applicable to your situation.

If you are employed by or directly representing the builder...

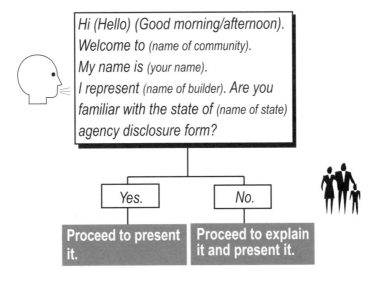

Hi (Hello) (Good morning/afternoon). Welcome to *(name of community)*. My name is *(your name)*. I represent *(name of builder)*. Are you familiar with the state of *(name of state)* agency disclosure form?

Yes. → Proceed to present it.

No. → Proceed to explain it and present it.

If you are employed by or associated with a real estate brokerage company representing one or several builders...

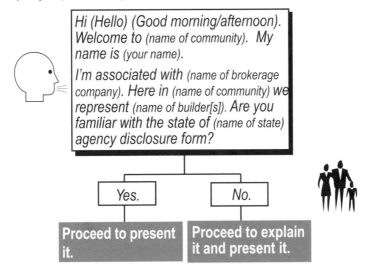

Hi (Hello) (Good morning/afternoon). Welcome to *(name of community)*. My name is *(your name)*.

I'm associated with *(name of brokerage company)*. Here in *(name of community)* we represent *(name of builder[s])*. Are you familiar with the state of *(name of state)* agency disclosure form?

Yes. → Proceed to present it.

No. → Proceed to explain it and present it.

Key

Customer response

Professional Communicator

Greeting/Welcome (Continued)

GW8. The Realtor "in a hurry" or "just previewing"

Situation

A Realtor (usually in for the first time) enters your sales arena with a customer in tow. It appears that he or she does not want you to get too close to the customer. The Realtor possibly stands between you and the customer, produces a business card (maybe), and introduces himself and his customers, possibly saying something like, "We're just previewing..."

Strategy

"Break the ice" by recognizing and complimenting the Realtor, welcoming him or her and the customer. Then, determine the frame of reference relative to the amount of time they have available.

Rationale

Realtors typically want to maintain total control over the customer and not allow you to do anything. With this strategy you can quickly connect with the Realtor. Don't use this technique if you already have a good, established relationship with the Realtor.

GW8. A Realtor (usually in for the first time) enters your sales arena with a customer in tow.

Hi (Hello) (Good morning/afternoon). Welcome to (name of community). My name is (your name) from (name of builder).

As the Realtor hands you a card, *quickly* observe the agent's first name.

It's good to see you*, (first name of Realtor).

Then turn to the customer and continue.

And you are?

Customers give their names.

Congratulations,(name of customers)! You are fortunate to be working with (first name of Realtor). By reputation, he (she) is one of the most knowledgeable real estate professionals in (name of your city or area).

Looking at both of them, then proceed with...

About how much time do you have to look at our models** today?

Wait for response. Then say...

No problem. In the (short) time you have, I'll make sure you get a brochure and see our model(s)**, but first I'd like to be helpful and take just a moment to give you a quick overview about (name of company), the location here at (name of community), our amenities, and our homes, OK?

*This is also an appropriate strategy to use with Realtors who visit frequently with customers. In these instances, it is good to say, "Nice to see you again."

**(or) homes (or) community (or) home sites, as the case may be.

Key
 Customer response   Professional Communicator

Greeting/Welcome *(Continued)*

GW9. The "they split up" scenario

Situation

Either at the beginning or during the course of a presentation, a couple splits up. One goes one way and the other goes another.

Strategy

Direct a statement to them with enthusiasm and a somewhat dramatic sense of flair, which should cause them to focus on you and your information for a few moments.

Rationale

Keep them together for just enough time for you to give them a quick overview; at least for the purpose of getting them started in the right direction before they begin their elimination process.

GW9. Either at the beginning or during the course of a presentation, a couple splits up. One goes one way and the other goes another.

Nodding your head with warmth and subtle enthusiasm.

(Name of customers), if you could kind of stick with me (stay with me) for just a few moments, I'd like to give you a quick overview about some of the unique features and benefits that (name of builder) includes in our homes. Then, please feel free to take as much time to look on your own as you would like. Would that be OK?

Key

Customer response — Professional Communicator

Discovery

Observations

Seek first to understand, then to be understood.

-Stephen R. Covey

To be able to ask a question clearly is two-thirds of the way to getting it answered.

-John Ruskin

Introduction

On the following pages you will find a specific situation, strategy, and rationale explained. The facing page shows the corresponding Smart Selling Technique.

Actual situations may vary slightly. You must apply your common sense and logic to use these techniques to their best advantage.

In this section

The following Smart Selling Techniques are used during the Discovery phase of the *Sequence for Success*.

SST	See page
D1. No sense of time	36
D2. Finding out their commitment	38
D3. Type of homes	40
D4. The empty nester customer	42
D5. Financial possibilities	44
D6. We want to see everything	46
D7. The price range	48
D8. Their present home	50
D9. Their primary reasons for looking	52
D10. Ability to take action	54

Discovery *(Continued)*

D1. No sense of time

Situation

During the greeting process, you have not yet found out how much time the customers perceive they have available.

Strategy

Ask.

Rationale

The customers' response will give you an indication of how you must pace your presentation.

D1. During the greeting process, you have not yet found out how much time the customers perceive they have available.

> (Name of customers), and about how much time do you have to look at our models* today?

**(or) homes (or) community (or) home sites, as the case may be.

New Home Specialist Inc.   37

Discovery *(Continued)*

D2. Finding out their commitment

Situation

After establishing rapport, smoothly and tactfully begin finding out the customers' commitment.

Strategy

Find out where the customers are in their process and where else they might have looked.

Rationale

You can gauge the customers' commitment by finding out how long they have been looking and whether they enjoy the "looking" process. You can then continue to gather more customer information based on answers to these questions.

D2. After establishing rapport, smoothly and tactfully begin finding out the customers' commitment.

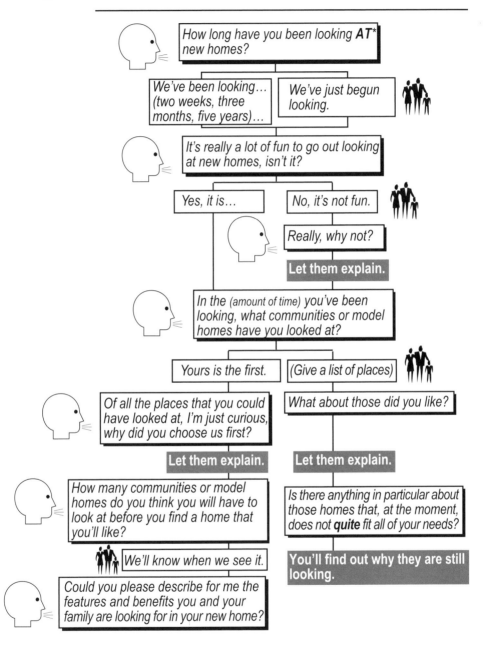

How long have you been looking AT new homes?*

We've been looking... (two weeks, three months, five years)...

We've just begun looking.

It's really a lot of fun to go out looking at new homes, isn't it?

Yes, it is...

No, it's not fun.

Really, why not?

Let them explain.

In the (amount of time) you've been looking, what communities or model homes have you looked at?

Yours is the first.

(Give a list of places)

Of all the places that you could have looked at, I'm just curious, why did you choose us first?

What about those did you like?

Let them explain.

Let them explain.

How many communities or model homes do you think you will have to look at before you find a home that you'll like?

Is there anything in particular about those homes that, at the moment, does not **quite** fit all of your needs?

We'll know when we see it.

You'll find out why they are still looking.

Could you please describe for me the features and benefits you and your family are looking for in your new home?

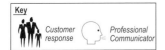

Key

Customer response

Professional Communicator

*It is very important to use the word AT rather than the word FOR.

Discovery *(Continued)*

D3. Type of homes

Situation

You want to discover what the customers might be interested in seeing.

Strategy

Ask.

Rationale

You want to find out if you have an opportunity that may work for the customers.

D3. You want to discover what the customers might be interested in seeing.

What type of homes have you been looking at?

(or)

What type of home are you considering?

(Customers describe what they have in mind.)	We don't know. We're just out looking.

When this occurs, you need to sort through it. Then proceed with...

Oh, what type of home do you have now?

Engage in a dialogue by encouraging them to tell you about features, location, etc. that they like or enjoy, by asking...

What features do you like best about it?

Again, let them tell you what they like. You will be finding out some "hot buttons" and what they might want in their new home.

Reply sincerely with...

It sounds like a very nice home...I'm just curious, if there is anything about your present home that you could change to make it ideal for your current situation (needs), what might that be?

Shut up and listen carefully.

Their response will probably be their primary "hot button." When they give you an answer, discuss it with them, and ask...

Is there anything else that you would like to change?

Key

Customer response — Professional Communicator

Discovery *(Continued)*

D4. The empty nester customers

Situation

You are working with "empty nester" customers.

Strategy

Cause the customers to think about and visualize (perhaps even for the first time) what might be some of the negatives of what they have now.

Rationale

You must help the customers feel discontented with their current situation since the one major competition that you might have with empty nesters is the home they already own and in which they reside.

D4. You are working with "empty nester" customers.

> *How long have you been living in your present home?*

If their answer is approximately five years or more, proceed to ask...

> *Has the neighborhood changed over the years?*
>
> **(or)**
>
> *How has the neighborhood changed over the years?*

Listen carefully to what they say. For example...

> *Oh, it's gone downhill. (or)*
>
> *When we first moved there, we knew all of our neighbors and now we hardly know anyone, etc.*

Engage in dialogue and direct your presentation of benefits toward those answers.

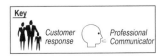

Key

Customer response

Professional Communicator

Discovery *(Continued)*

D5. Financial possibilities

Situation

You want to discover the customers' financial possibilities.

Strategy

Ask.

Rationale

This is a prequalification technique.

D5. You want to discover the customers' financial possibilities.

Our homes range from *(state lowest amount)* to *(state highest amount)*, depending on the size of the home you select, the location, and the amount of customization (personalization) you choose to do. What would you like to see first today?

Discovery *(Continued)*

D6. We want to see everything

Situation

You have a wide range in price and many homes to offer and show.

Strategy

Get customers to commit to a specific amount of time, and then to easily "eliminate" what they probably don't want to see.

Rationale

Customers shop by the process of elimination.

D6. You have a wide range in price and many homes to offer and show.

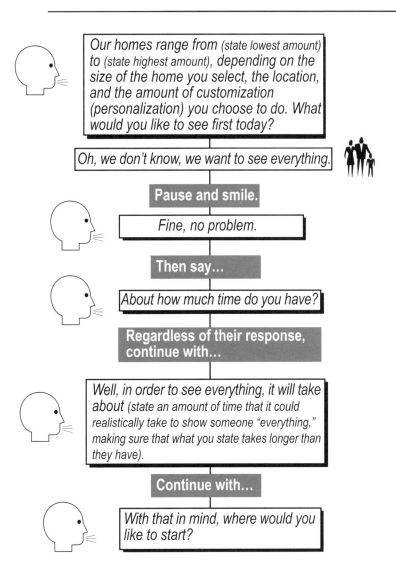

> *Our homes range from* (state lowest amount) *to* (state highest amount), *depending on the size of the home you select, the location, and the amount of customization (personalization) you choose to do. What would you like to see first today?*

Oh, we don't know, we want to see everything.

Pause and smile.

Fine, no problem.

Then say...

About how much time do you have?

Regardless of their response, continue with...

Well, in order to see everything, it will take about (state an amount of time that it could realistically take to show someone "everything," making sure that what you state takes longer than they have).

Continue with...

With that in mind, where would you like to start?

Key

Customer response — Professional Communicator

Discovery *(Continued)*

D7. The price range

Situation

Customers indicate that their "price range" is below what you have to offer. For example, your homes start at $200,000, but the customers say, "we didn't want to go over $180,000."

Strategy

Find out exactly how they have determined their "price ceiling."

Rationale

This is a prequalification technique.

D7. Customers indicate that their "price range" is below what you have to offer. For example, your homes start at $200,000, but the customers say, "we didn't want to go over $180,000."

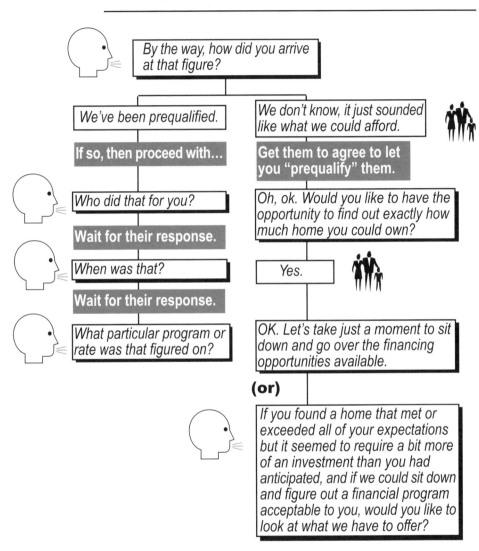

(or)

Discovery *(Continued)*

D8. Their present home

Situation

You don't know if the customers currently own or rent a home.

Strategy

Discover if ownership of their present home or a lease on a rental home will pose an obstacle in their buying process.

Rationale

You want to establish the urgency of their buying decision.

D8. You don't know if the customers currently own or rent a home.

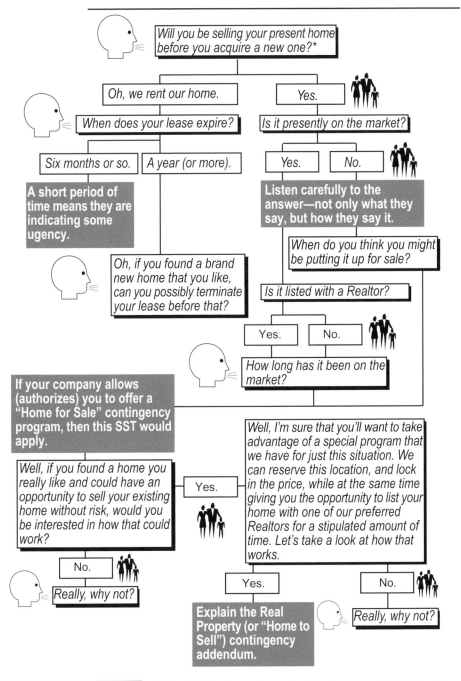

*This SST replaces the typical industry psychobabble "Do you have to sell your house?"

Discovery *(Continued)*

D9. Their primary reasons for looking

Situation

You want to discover the customers' primary reason for looking.

Strategy

Ask.

Rationale

Understanding customers' primary reason for looking allows you to gauge their motivation level.

D9. You want to discover the customers' primary reason for looking.

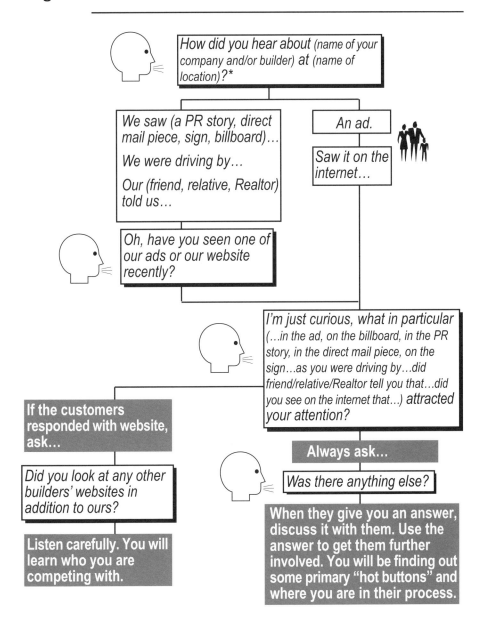

How did you hear about (name of your company and/or builder) *at* (name of location)?*

We saw (a PR story, direct mail piece, sign, billboard)…

We were driving by…

Our (friend, relative, Realtor) told us…

An ad.

Saw it on the internet…

Oh, have you seen one of our ads or our website recently?

I'm just curious, what in particular (…in the ad, on the billboard, in the PR story, in the direct mail piece, on the sign…as you were driving by…did friend/relative/Realtor tell you that…did you see on the internet that…) *attracted your attention?*

If the customers responded with website, ask…

Did you look at any other builders' websites in addition to ours?

Listen carefully. You will learn who you are competing with.

Always ask…

Was there anything else?

When they give you an answer, discuss it with them. Use the answer to get them further involved. You will be finding out some primary "hot buttons" and where you are in their process.

Key

Customer response

Professional Communicator

*This SST replaces the typical industry psychobabble "What brings you out here today?"

Discovery *(Continued)*

D10. Ability to take action

Situation

You want to discover the customers' ability to take action.

Strategy

Ask.

Rationale

You want to find out what their time frame is for making a purchase decision.

D10.You want to discover the customers' ability to take action.

When you find a home you like, when do you think you'll be moving into it?*

Key

Customer response | Professional Communicator

*This SST replaces the typical industry psychobabble "What's your time frame?" or "When do you think you'll be doin' something? "

Demonstration/Selection

Observations

If you've got it, flaunt it.

-Mae West

*If you can get them to **own it**, they will **buy it**.*

-Tom Hopkins

Introduction

On the following pages you will find a specific situation, strategy, and rationale explained. The facing page shows the corresponding Smart Selling Technique.

Actual situations may vary slightly. You must apply your common sense and logic to use these techniques to their best advantage.

In this section

The following SSTs are used during the Demonstration/ Selection phase of the *Sequence for Success*.

continued on the next page

Demonstration/Selection *(Continued)*

In this section *(continued)*

Demonstration/Selection (Continued)

DS1. The telephone interruption

Situation

During the presentation, the telephone rings and the customer says, "Oh, go ahead and answer it."

Strategy

Maintain control of the presentation and do not get sidetracked. Always turn the ringer volume off.

Rationale

Never allow the telephone to interrupt you during a presentation. If you are working alone, use an answering device.

DS1. During the presentation, the telephone rings and the customer says, "Oh, go ahead and answer it."

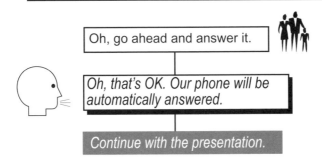

Oh, go ahead and answer it.

Oh, that's OK. Our phone will be automatically answered.

Continue with the presentation.

Suggested messages for the answering machine or voice mail

Message:

Thank you for calling (Name of community). Our models are open from _____ to _____ daily. If you have called during open hours, our representatives are busy with customers right now. Your call is important to us, so at the tone, please leave your name, phone number, and a message, and your call will be returned as quickly as possible. Thank you.

Key

Customer response

Professional Communicator

Demonstration/Selection *(Continued)*

DS2. On their own

Situation

You are attempting to accompany the customers to your first model home and the customers indicate that they want to go on their own.

Strategy

Agree with the customers while letting them know that you are not trying to control or pressure them in any way. At the same time, attempt to get their concurrence for you to give them a quick overview of what you have available.

Rationale

Maintain control of the demonstration/selection process.

DS2. You are attempting to accompany the customers to your first model home and the customers indicate that they want to go on their own.

(Name of customers) I sense that you want to look at the models alone, and I respect that. So please feel free to do that... (Slight pause)...but if it would be all right with you, I'd like to just accompany you to the first model, and, on the way, give you a quick overview about some of the unique exterior and interior features that you will see, and cover what's included with our homes.

Nodding head with warmth and subtle enthusiasm.

Key

Customer response

Professional Communicator

Demonstration/Selection *(Continued)*

DS3. The distracted customer

Situation

During the course of a presentation, you find that the customers' attention seems to have drifted.

Strategy

Subtly regain the customers' attention without appearing to be controlling. This is accomplished by using a communication tactic that is designed to interrupt their expectation. It is called the *intentional pause*. Upon seeing any evidence of distraction or the customers not paying attention, simply begin a statement that contains information that should have some level of interest. While verbalizing the statement, begin to slowly, distinctly, and gradually increase the speed of your speech and volume, ending abruptly on an important word. Within seconds you should have their attention.

Rationale

The sudden absence of sound is more dramatic than its constant presence.

DS3. During the course of a presentation, you find that the customers' attention seems to have drifted.

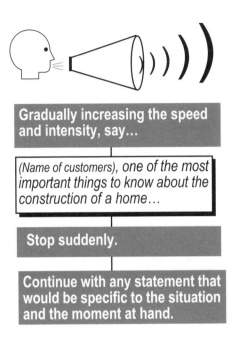

Gradually increasing the speed and intensity, say...

(Name of customers), one of the most important things to know about the construction of a home...

Stop suddenly.

Continue with any statement that would be specific to the situation and the moment at hand.

Key

Customer response

Professional Communicator

Demonstration/Selection *(Continued)*

DS4. Know it all

Situation

When you start to tell the customers about your company or location, etc., they say that they know all about the company, location, etc.

Strategy

Find out what or how much the customers know.

Rationale

You want to make sure that customers have accurate knowledge.

DS4. When you start to tell the customers about your company or location, etc., they say that they know all about the company, location, etc.

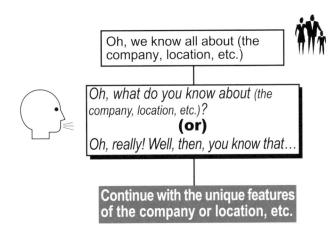

Oh, we know all about (the company, location, etc.)

Oh, *what do you know about* (the company, location, etc.)?
(or)
Oh, really! Well, then, you know that...

Continue with the unique features of the company or location, etc.

Key

Customer response

Professional Communicator

Demonstration/Selection *(Continued)*

DS5. Running interference

Situation

You are working with customers and their Realtor, parents, or some other "expert" who is accompanying them is interfering.

Strategy

Establish an environment in which you can direct your presentation to the real buyers, while still respecting and recognizing the importance of the person(s) accompanying them.

Rationale

Do this at the first sign of *negative* interference but with warmth and sincerity to maintain control of the process. "It takes two people to make an argument and the sales person should never be one of them." Remember, never argue or debate, but rather always persuade.

DS5. You are working with customers and their Realtor, parents, or some other "expert" who is accompanying them is interfering.

(Name of person who is interjecting), *that's an interesting question (idea, concept, etc.).*

Then proceed to handle their question or objection as you would any objection, using the Six Step Method^SM

Key

Customer response · Professional Communicator

Demonstration/Selection *(Continued)*

DS6. Total square footage

Situation

When stating the "square footage" of any specific home, use the **total** square footage first, followed by the **actual** living space.

Strategy

Position your homes using all "square footage" that is actually built and, therefore, provided. Describe the **total** square footage while at the same time always being technically and legally correct.

Rationale

It costs money to build all the square footage whether it is the garage, porch, or living space. Most customers only use the climate-controlled space when calculating price-per-square-foot. By not including the **total** space, they get a false figure.

DS6. When stating the "square footage" of any specific home, use the total square footage first, followed by the actual living space.

Our (name of model) is approximately (state total amount of square feet, including garage, basement, porches, etc.) of which (state actual number of square feet that is climate-controlled living space) is living space, with the rest devoted to a (#) car garage*, storage*, porches*, and finishable basement space.*

* use appropriate examples.

Demonstration/Selection *(Continued)*

DS7. Smaller square footage

Situation

You are selling "smaller square footage than competitors," but you have custom features, etc. that cause your price-per-square-foot to be higher than theirs.

Strategy

Cause the customer to quickly experience that your design, quality, and amenities far offset a *cheaper* price-per-square-foot. (This technique doesn't work if your design is boring or ordinary.)

Rationale

Price-per-square-foot is a misleading criteria for comparing homes.

DS7. You are selling "smaller square footage than a competitor," but you have custom features, etc. that cause your price-per-square-foot to be higher than theirs.

With warmth and sincerity, say...

We don't build just a big basic box with a lot of square footage as cheaply as possible. Rather, we pay attention to things like architectural detail, quality, craftsmanship, and a design concept to make your home unique.

You know, there are a lot of ways to cut corners when building a house to lower the price. I don't know what other builders do, but I can tell you about (name of company's) commitment to customer satisfaction and how our homes are designed and constructed. Our value is in the total package.

Key

Customer response — Professional Communicator

Demonstration/Selection *(Continued)*

DS8. Obtain feedback and recap

Situation

Always use a transition statement before you accompany the customers (or they go) from the sales/information center or office to the models, home sites, or completed homes.

Strategy

Obtain feedback. Find out the customers' level of interest to open the door and to make it easy for them to ask questions.

Rationale

Some customers may be reluctant to "ask questions" for fear of appearing ignorant or too interested. An unasked question is an unanswered question. An unanswered question is incomplete information. Incomplete information means you won't connect all the "dots."

DS8. Always use a transition statement before you accompany the customers (or they go) from the sales/information center or office.

(Name of customers), before we (you) go to to see the models*, do you have any questions about *(name of builder)*, the location here at *(name of community)*, the amenities, or is there anything else of importance to you that we have not yet covered?

*(or) homes (or) community (or) home sites, as the case may be.

Demonstration/Selection *(Continued)*

DS9. Seed of doubt

Situation

During the presentation, you have the opportunity to present a design or construction feature that is unique or special.

Strategy

Position your unique selling position (USP) and plant a seed of doubt.

Rationale

Establish the value of your homes and set them apart from the competition by having the customers experience the benefit of your USP and cause them to understand that other builders do not offer this USP.

DS9. During the presentation, you have the opportunity to present a design or construction feature that is unique or special.

(Customer's name), although it is not required by any building code, we provide (state a specific construction USP and its benefit to the customer). I don't know why all builders don't (state what the USP is), but we do it because we believe it's the right thing to do.

Example:

We build our homes with the exterior wall studs 18 inches on center, instead of 24 inches on center. This makes the walls sturdier, more durable, and provides for smoother interior finishing.

Example:

We use the services of a licensed engineer during the course of construction to inspect and certify that all aspects of construction meet or exceed expectations. This gives you third-party assurance, (customer's name), that the quality of construction and the process meet or exceed all requirements.

Key
Customer response
Professional Communicator

NOTE: You can only use this SST if your builder is the ONLY one doing it in your area. The USP must be unique.

Demonstration/Selection *(Continued)*

DS10. High expectations

Situation

You are going to show a spectacular view from a particular area of a home, or some exceptional custom feature in a home.

Strategy

Before demonstrating, pique the customers' interest and establish or "set up" a **high** expectation level.

Rationale

You want to generate emotional involvement with the home and its features and benefits.

DS10. You are going to show a spectacular view from a particular area of a home, or some exceptional custom feature in a home.

> Before we go into this home, I just want to tell you about the (...spectacular/great/fantastic...) view of the (state the focal point of view) that we are going to see from the (room or area).
>
> **(or)**
>
> In the (room or area), you are going to see a (state the focal point of custom or unique design feature).

Demonstration/Selection *(Continued)*

DS11. No existing homes available

Situation

You have only homes-to-be-built in the future with **no** existing homes available for immediate or near-term occupancy.

Strategy

Early in the presentation, present the benefit and advantages of having a home built-to-order. Incorporate this SST into the first several minutes of your planned presentation to establish customers' expectations.

Rationale

Plant a seed that will cause the customers to *think* about the benefits and the possibility of waiting to have a home built for them.

DS11. You have only homes-to-be-built in the future with no existing homes available for immediate or near-term occupancy.

> Our research has shown that, when given a choice, most people prefer to have their brand new home built exclusively for them and personalized to their taste, rather than to settle for a house that has been built to meet someone else's requirements. Have you thought about that?

Pause and wait for their response.

Key

Customer response

Professional Communicator

Demonstration/Selection *(Continued)*

DS12. Undecorated or non-merchandised home

Situation

You are going to show an undecorated or non-merchandised completed home after showing a decorated or merchandised home.

Strategy

Before demonstrating, establish or "set up" the customers' expectation level.

Rationale

Avoid almost certain disappointment when the customers see an undecorated or non-merchandised home.

DS12. You are going to show an undecorated or non-merchandised completed home after showing a decorated or merchandised home.

*(Name of customers), the home that we are going to see, unlike the model, will not have all the furniture and decorator items. To your advantage, you will see this home as it will be completed for you when you move in. And, as you look through it, you can also visualize how **you** might decorate it.*

If the home you are going to show the customers is a "flipped" version or reverse of the model, add...

Also, this home you will see shows architectural diversity in that it is a reverse of the model.

Key

Customer response

Professional Communicator

Demonstration/Selection *(Continued)*

DS13. Home under construction

Situation

You are going to show a home ***under construction*** that may have construction trash, piles of dirt in the yard, water in the bathtub or in the basement, or some other common construction dilemma.

Strategy

Before demonstrating, establish or "set up" the customers' expectation level by identifying the "dilemma."

Rationale

By being proactive, you avoid disappointment when the customers see construction debris.

DS13. You are going to show a home under construction that may have construction trash.

> Since the home we are going to see is under construction, sometimes it is quite common during construction and before the home is completed, to have, for instance, *(state what the "dilemma" might be)*. This, of course, is always completely and properly taken care of before any of our homes are completed for a homeowner.

Key

Customer response

Professional Communicator

Demonstration/Selection *(Continued)*

DS14. Warranty

Situation

You want the customers to understand the value of buying a home from your builder(s).

Strategy

State the warranty coverage provided by the builder(s).

Rationale

One of buyers' six hidden fears is doing business with a builder. Explaining the warranty addresses that fear.

DS14. You want the customers to understand the value of buying a home from your builder(s).

(Name of customers), (name of company) is so committed to customer satisfaction that we put our commitment in writing.

If your company provides the buyers with an extended and insured warranty, continue with...

And, further, we back it up with *(#)* years of insured warranty protection provided by *(Full Name of Warranty Company—don't use abbreviations), which* is included with all of our homes, and transferable in the event you should sell your home in the future.

Key

Customer response

Professional Communicator

Demonstration/Selection *(Continued)*

DS15. Financing

Situation

You use a variety of outside sources for your customers' financing.

Strategy

Explain how easy it is to own one of your homes.

Rationale

One of the six hidden fears is the financing process. Explaining your mortgage process eliminates that fear.

DS15. You use a variety of outside sources for your customers' financing.

 Over the years, we have established a fine working relationship with some of the area's leading financial institutions. One of their representatives (use a name and title, if possible) *will be happy to meet with you—at your convenience—to go over the variety of great plans that we have available and to assist you in making the mortgage process very easy.*

If your company is affiliated with a financial institution or mortgage company, or has its own mortgage department, affiliate, or subsidiary company, say...

 As part of our total commitment to customer satisfaction, (name of builder) *has a mortgage services department* (affiliate, subsidiary, etc.) *called* (name of dept, affiliate, subsidiary, etc.). *One of their representatives* (use a name and title, if possible) *will be happy to meet with you—at your convenience—to go over a variety of great plans that we have available and to assist you in making the mortgage process very easy.*

NOTE: make absolutely sure that you include any language required by law for the purposes of required RESPA or other disclosure.

Demonstration/Selection *(Continued)*

DS16. Options or upgrades

Situation

You have a model(s) that contains many options or upgrades not included in the published or advertised price.

Strategy

Present the range of value for each model, from the lowest to the highest available, while stating the specific value (price) of the model that customers will see—including the options that could be purchased as shown.

Rationale

Buyers do not like to be "nickeled and dimed" or to become victims of what they perceive to be a "bait and switch" situation.

DS16. You have a model(s) that contains many options or upgrades not included in the published or advertised price.

The model(s) we are going to see is available from (state the lowest value) to (state the highest value). The actual version of the (name of specific model) is (state price with all options as shown), which includes the additional custom features that I will point out, except, of course, for the furnishings and decorator items.

Suggestion: create a well-designed placard to put on an easel and place in the foyer of the model that states:

Welcome to the *(Name of Model)*: *(#)* Bedrooms, *(#)* Baths, etc. This home is available from *(absolute lowest possible price—standard home site, no options)* to *(highest possible price—most expensive home site with all the options)*, depending on the location you select and the amount of customization (personalization) you choose to do.

This *(Name of Model)* as shown is $_____, which includes the following additional custom features (except, of course, for the furnishings and other decorator items not specifically listed):

(List all the optional features that are displayed, except, of course, for the furnishings and items that could be purchased.)

Key
Customer response
Professional Communicator

Demonstration/Selection *(Continued)*

DS17. Looking at resales

Situation

The customers say that they are also looking at resales.

Strategy

Cause the customers to think about what a "resale" really is.

Rationale

For most home builders, the resale market is your biggest competition. Accentuate the value of a brand new home and plant a seed of doubt.

DS17. The customers say that they are also looking at resales.

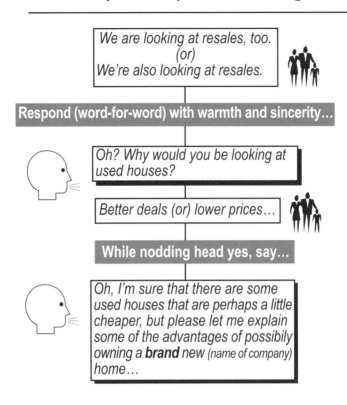

We are looking at resales, too.
(or)
We're also looking at resales.

Respond (word-for-word) with warmth and sincerity...

Oh? Why would you be looking at used houses?

Better deals (or) lower prices...

While nodding head yes, say...

Oh, I'm sure that there are some used houses that are perhaps a little cheaper, but please let me explain some of the advantages of possibily owning a **brand** new (name of company) home...

Additional SST

Our research has shown that when given a choice most people prefer to have their brand new home built exclusively for them and personalized to their taste, rather than to settle for a house that has been built to meet someone else's requirements. Have you thought about that?

Pause and wait for their response.

Key
Customer response
Professional Communicator

NOTE: Do not use this technique if the customers are accompanied by a Realtor that you do not know very well.

Demonstration/Selection *(Continued)*

DS18. Asking for the impossible

Situation

The customers ask for something or about something that you cannot provide (e.g., low prices, boat slips, tennis courts, etc.) or raise an objection you can't change.

Strategy

Feed back the customers' requests using extremes. Do not answer the question directly with a "No." Let the customers minimize the request or objection themselves.

Rationale

Find out on a "scale of 1 to 10" (1 = not important; 10 = absolutely must have, won't buy without) how important the request or objection is to the customers. When you add words like critically, vitally, or extremely, it causes the customers to give a knee-jerk (quick) response to the word. Typically the customers will say, "well, it's not CRITICAL, but I'd like it," or "well, it's not VITAL, but it would be really nice." If the response is on the low end of the scale, it won't keep them from buying.

DS18. The customers ask for something or about something that you cannot provide or raise an objection you can't change.

Well, this community doesn't have tennis courts. (or)
Oh, this house doesn't have a boat slip. (or)
We have to have a 3-car garage.

Is having tennis courts **critically** important to you? **(or)**

Is it **extremely** important to have a boat slip in the backyard? **(or)**

Is having a 3-car garage **vital** to you?

Listen carefully to their response.

Demonstration/Selection *(Continued)*

DS19. Federal violation

Situation

The customers ask questions such as, "What kind of people live here?" or "What's the ethnic make up of the neighborhood?"

Strategy

Be tactful with your answer and maintain a positive attitude.

Rationale

Make absolutely sure that you don't violate federal law.

DS19. The customers ask questions such as, "What kind of people live here?" or "What's the ethnic make up of the neighborhood?"

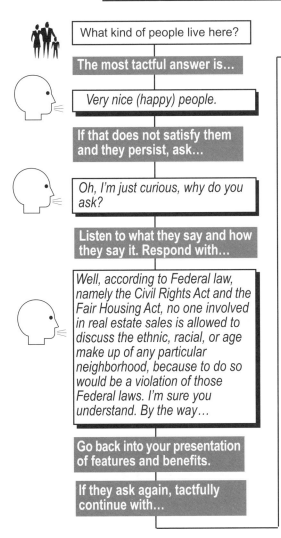

What kind of people live here?

The most tactful answer is...

Very nice (happy) people.

If that does not satisfy them and they persist, ask...

Oh, I'm just curious, why do you ask?

Listen to what they say and how they say it. Respond with...

Well, according to Federal law, namely the Civil Rights Act and the Fair Housing Act, no one involved in real estate sales is allowed to discuss the ethnic, racial, or age make up of any particular neighborhood, because to do so would be a violation of those Federal laws. I'm sure you understand. By the way...

Go back into your presentation of features and benefits.

If they ask again, tactfully continue with...

I'm sorry, but as I told you before, everyone involved in real estate sales is prohibited by law to discuss the ethnic, racial, or age make up of any particular neighborhood, because to do so would be a violation of those Federal laws. I'm sure you wouldn't want **us** to break the law, would you?

If they persist a third time, proceed, very tactfully, with...

I have answered your question twice to the extent allowed by law. May I ask you, are you a member or representative of any federal, state, or local government agency, or any civil rights enforcement group?

If they are, they will have to disclose it. If they say yes, respond with...

Great! How'd I do?

Wait for their response. Remember they have to live somewhere, too, so then proceed with...

Good, which one of our homes would you like to own?

Key

Customer response

Professional Communicator

Demonstration/Selection *(Continued)*

DS20. Occupying your time

Situation

Previous buyers are unwittingly occupying your time during peak selling opportunities (typically on weekends).

Strategy

Inform the customers how important they are and *tactfully* establish an expectation level for your future service and involvement. You want your customers to feel valued and for you to keep them happy and a source of referrals.

Rationale

Your primary objective on busy weekends is to be face-to-face with people who do not yet own one of your homes.

NOTE: This should be presented with warmth and sincerity **after** the customers approve the agreement and **before** they leave.

DS20. Previous buyers are unwittingly occupying your time during peak selling opportunities (typically on weekends).

(Name of customers), I'm sure that between now and the time you move into your new home, you will probably have lots of questions, and I'll always be happy to do my best to answer them for you. So that I can give you my undivided attention and the quality time you deserve, please call me at any time so that we can schedule an appointment.

And by the way, if you should just happen to "drop in" some day and you find me busy with customers or on the phone, I know you won't be offended and will understand if I'm not able to spend a lot of time with you, OK?

Alternate SST

When you have an associate/ partner (assistant)* and want to avoid having customers unwittingly occupy your time during peak selling or Follow-Through¤ opportunities.

(Name of customers), I'm sure that between now and the time you move into your new home, you will probably have lots of questions, so I'd like you to meet my associate (state associate's name) because one of us will always try to be available to do our best to answer them for you. So that we can give you the quality time you deserve, call either of us at any time and we will schedule an appointment so that we can give you our undivided attention.

And by the way, if you should just happen to "drop in" some day and you find me busy with customers or on the phone, I know you won't be offended and will understand if I'm not able to spend a lot of time with you, but I can assure you that you will find (name of associate) to be extremely competent, capable, and always willing to help.

*Involve your associate/partner (assistant) at the earliest possible and appropriate time. Establish the expectation level for his or her future relationship, involvement, and participation with the customer.

Key
Customer response
Professional Communicator

Closing

Observations

Closing is selling.

-Tom Hopkins

The sale is made in the presentation. It is only lost if you fail to close or close improperly.

–Bob Schultz

Introduction

On the following pages you will find a specific situation, strategy, and rationale explained. The facing page shows the corresponding Smart Selling Technique.

Actual situations may vary slightly. You must apply your common sense and logic to use these techniques to their best advantage.

In this section

The following Smart Selling Techniques are used during the Closing phase of the *Sequence for Success*.

continued on the next page

Closing *(Continued)*

In this section *(continued)*

Closing (Continued)

C1. After the first

Situation

Immediately after you show or demonstrate the very first model, floor plan, home site, open house, or completed home.

Strategy

Pose discovery questions while at the same time asking for the sale by qualifying the customers' choice or preference.

Rationale

People shop using the process of elimination. We want to consciously take them through that process. A customer's response to any question will be a decision—Yes, No, Maybe. These first three techniques lead the customer through the process of elimination.

C1. Immediately after you show or demonstrate the very first model, floor plan, home site, open house, or completed home.

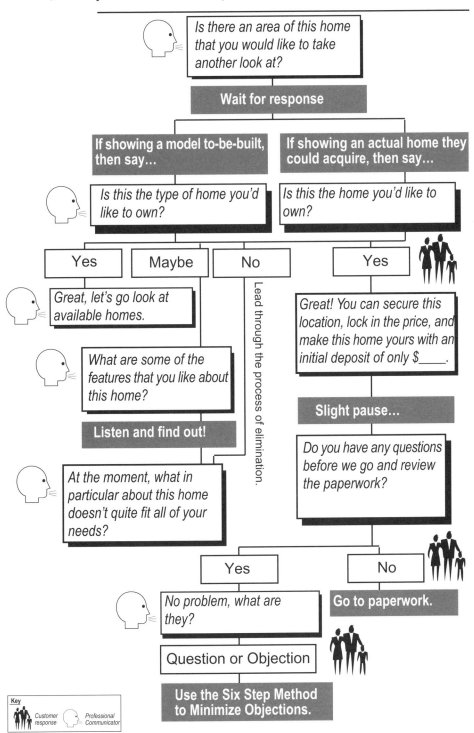

Is there an area of this home that you would like to take another look at?

Wait for response

If showing a model to-be-built, then say...

Is this the type of home you'd like to own?

If showing an actual home they could acquire, then say...

Is this the home you'd like to own?

| Yes | Maybe | No | Yes |

Great, let's go look at available homes.

Lead through the process of elimination.

What are some of the features that you like about this home?

Listen and find out!

At the moment, what in particular about this home doesn't quite fit all of your needs?

Great! You can secure this location, lock in the price, and make this home yours with an initial deposit of only $____.

Slight pause...

Do you have any questions before we go and review the paperwork?

| Yes | No |

No problem, what are they?

Go to paperwork.

Question or Objection

Use the Six Step Method to Minimize Objections.

Key
Customer response
Professional Communicator

Closing (Continued)

C2. After the second

Situation

Immediately after you show or demonstrate the second model, floor plan, home site, open house, or completed home.

Strategy

Pose discovery questions while at the same time asking for the sale by qualifying their choice or preference.

Rationale

Continue to lead the prospect further along the process of elimination.

C2. Immediately after you show or demonstrate the second model, floor plan, home site, open house, or completed home.

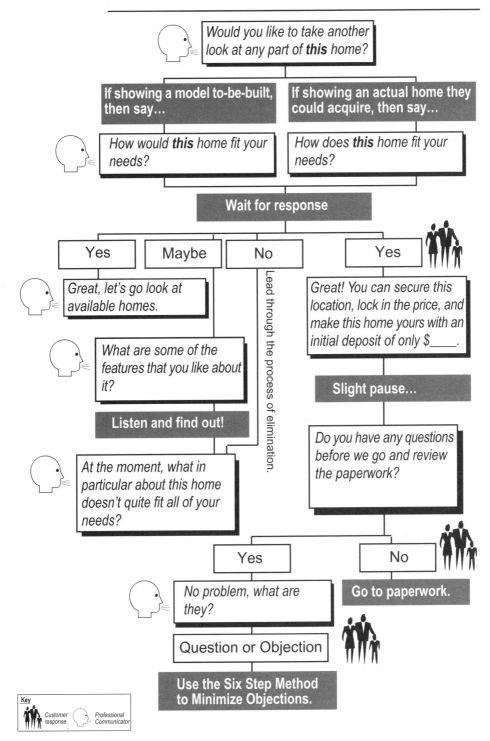

Would you like to take another look at any part of **this** home?

If showing a model to-be-built, then say...

If showing an actual home they could acquire, then say...

How would **this** home fit your needs?

How does **this** home fit your needs?

Wait for response

| Yes | Maybe | No | Yes |

Lead through the process of elimination.

Great, let's go look at available homes.

What are some of the features that you like about it?

Listen and find out!

At the moment, what in particular about this home doesn't quite fit all of your needs?

Great! You can secure this location, lock in the price, and make this home yours with an initial deposit of only $____.

Slight pause...

Do you have any questions before we go and review the paperwork?

| Yes | No |

No problem, what are they?

Go to paperwork.

Question or Objection

Use the Six Step Method to Minimize Objections.

Key

Customer response

Professional Communicator

Closing *(Continued)*

C3. After the third

Situation

Immediately after you show the third model, floor plan, home site, open house, or completed home.

Strategy

Pose discovery questions while at the same time asking for the sale by qualifying their choice or preference.

Rationale

By continuing to provide choices and asking for decisions, you help to take the customer through the process of elimination. Never show more than three of anything without using this technique.

C3. Immediately after you show the third model, floor plan, home site, open house, or completed home.

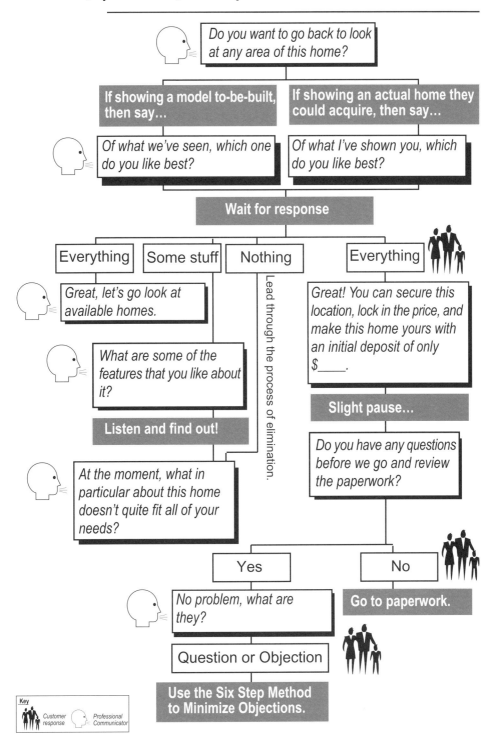

Do you want to go back to look at any area of this home?

If showing a model to-be-built, then say...

If showing an actual home they could acquire, then say...

Of what we've seen, which one do you like best?

Of what I've shown you, which do you like best?

Wait for response

| Everything | Some stuff | Nothing | Everything |

Great, let's go look at available homes.

What are some of the features that you like about it?

Listen and find out!

At the moment, what in particular about this home doesn't quite fit all of your needs?

Lead through the process of elimination.

Great! You can secure this location, lock in the price, and make this home yours with an initial deposit of only $____.

Slight pause...

Do you have any questions before we go and review the paperwork?

| Yes | No |

No problem, what are they?

Go to paperwork.

Question or Objection

Use the Six Step Method to Minimize Objections.

Key

Customer response — Professional Communicator

Closing *(Continued)*

C4. We liked everything

Situation

When you ask, "Of what I've shown you (or) of what you've seen, which home did you like best," the customers say, "Oh, we don't know, we liked everything."

Strategy

Agree that all of the homes are very nice and continue to lead the customers through the process of elimination.

Rationale

Restate your question and get the customers to eliminate the home(s) they don't really like as much.

NOTE: Only use this Smart Selling Technique if you have established a good rapport with the customer. This technique must be presented with good-natured humor.

C4. The customers say, "Oh, we don't know, we liked everything."

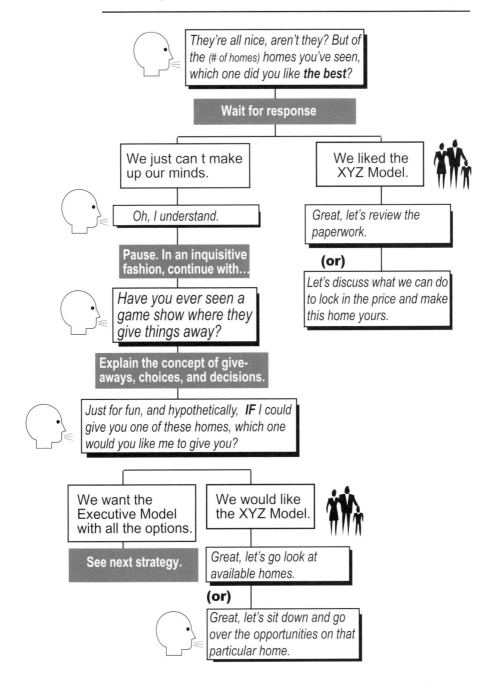

*They're all nice, aren't they? But of the (# of homes) homes you've seen, which one did you like **the best**?*

Wait for response

We just can t make up our minds.

We liked the XYZ Model.

Oh, I understand.

Great, let's review the paperwork.

(or)

Let's discuss what we can do to lock in the price and make this home yours.

Pause. In an inquisitive fashion, continue with...

Have you ever seen a game show where they give things away?

Explain the concept of give-aways, choices, and decisions.

*Just for fun, and hypothetically, **IF** I could give you one of these homes, which one would you like me to give you?*

We want the Executive Model with all the options.

We would like the XYZ Model.

See next strategy.

Great, let's go look at available homes.

(or)

Great, let's sit down and go over the opportunities on that particular home.

Key

Customer response

Professional Communicator

Closing *(Continued)*

C5. The most expensive model

Situation

After asking the customers which home they would like in a hypothetical game show scenario, the customers respond by picking the most expensive model.

Strategy

Use the process of elimination to further cause a decision.

Rationale

They might, since you are "giving it away," choose the biggest or most expensive, but nonetheless, you will have caused a decision.

C5. The customers respond by picking the most expensive model.

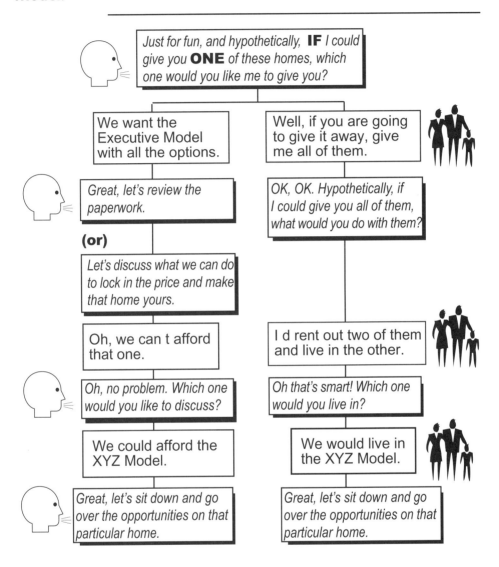

*Just for fun, and hypothetically, **IF** I could give you **ONE** of these homes, which one would you like me to give you?*

We want the Executive Model with all the options.

Great, let's review the paperwork.

(or)

Let's discuss what we can do to lock in the price and make that home yours.

Oh, we can t afford that one.

Oh, no problem. Which one would you like to discuss?

We could afford the XYZ Model.

Great, let's sit down and go over the opportunities on that particular home.

Well, if you are going to give it away, give me all of them.

OK, OK. Hypothetically, if I could give you all of them, what would you do with them?

I d rent out two of them and live in the other.

Oh that's smart! Which one would you live in?

We would live in the XYZ Model.

Great, let's sit down and go over the opportunities on that particular home.

Closing *(Continued)*

C6. Unaccompanied customers

Situation

Unaccompanied customers return to your sales office from the models.

Strategy

Pose a discovery question while at the same time asking for the sale by qualifying their choice or preference.

Rationale

Even if you did not have the opportunity to show or demonstrate a model, floor plan, home site, open house, or completed home, you can still guide the customers through the process of elimination.

C6. Unaccompanied customers return to your sales office from the models.

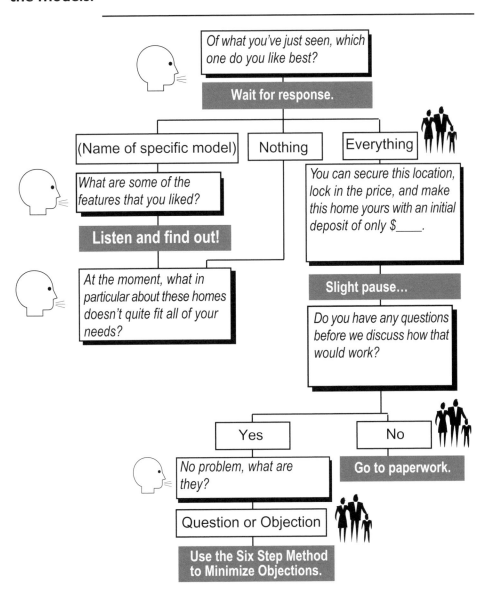

Of what you've just seen, which one do you like best?

Wait for response.

(Name of specific model) | Nothing | Everything

What are some of the features that you liked?

Listen and find out!

At the moment, what in particular about these homes doesn't quite fit all of your needs?

You can secure this location, lock in the price, and make this home yours with an initial deposit of only $____.

Slight pause...

Do you have any questions before we discuss how that would work?

Yes | No

No problem, what are they?

Go to paperwork.

Question or Objection

Use the Six Step Method to Minimize Objections.

Key

Customer response | Professional Communicator

Closing *(Continued)*

C7. To-Be-Built

Situation

You are showing a model or plan **to-be-built.** Site more—Sell more.

Strategy

Always lead the customer to the home site.

Sales and, therefore, compensation will increase in direct proportion to the number of interested and qualified people that you take to a home site.

Rationale

Scarcity creates urgency. In either situation (Yes/Maybe or No), the customer is making a decision. Your response is to discover the objection and use the Six Step Method to Minimize Objections.

Home Site Matrix

This Home Site Matrix enables you to divide available home sites into smaller categories based on specific characteristics. Once in smaller groups, you can create a sense of scarcity based on the unique selling proposition of the sites. Scarcity creates urgency. Urgency leads to sales.

continued on the next page

C7. You are showing a model or plan to-be-built. Site more—Sell more.

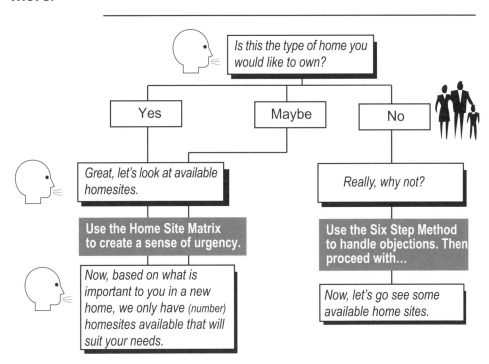

Closing *(Continued)*

Home Site Matrix *(continued)*

Follow these steps to use the Home Site Matrix to assist you in finding a fit for each individual customer.

Step	Action
1	Complete the Home Site Matrix tool for every available home site on which you can sell a home to-be-built. Once you have established the Unique Selling Proposition (USP) of each, chart the home sites on the matrix.
2	Using your discovery questioning skills, establish your customers' ▶ Unique tastes, ▶ Preferences, ▶ Lifestyle, or ▶ Requirements.
3	Establish several options for each customer to review.
4	Take the interested customers ONLY to those home sites that best fit their unique tastes, preferences, lifestyle, or requirements.
5	Try not to show more than three options.
6	Allow the customers to touch, feel, and see the site to increase the probability of bringing the presentation to a final close.

Home Site Matrix™

Complete one form per available home site. After establishing a customer's unique tastes, preferences, lifestyle, or requirements, you can narrow the number of prospective home sites that will fit the customer.

Home Site Identification

Section _____   **Price*** _____ (*relative as a % to average)

Lot _____

Block _____

Unique Selling Proposition

Site Characteristics

Location	Size*	Shape	View	Orientation	Topography
○ Entry way	○ Small	○ Pie	○ Water	○ Sun	○ Level
○ Collector	○ Medium	○ Square	○ Golf	○ Wind	○ Sloped
○ Cul-de-sac	○ Large	○ Odd	○ Park	○ North	○ Trees
○ Dead end	○ X-large	○ Long	○ Pool	○ South	○ Shrubs
○ Alley	(*relative to	○ Wide	○ Scenic	○ East	○ Rocks
	standard site)	○ Narrow	○ Other	○ West	

Site Constraints

Easements	Home Limitations	Other
○ Utility boxes	○ Exterior elevation	○ _____
○ Fire hydrants	○ Size of home	○ _____
○ Street lights	○ Only model _____	○ _____

Cultural Considerations

House #s	Positioning	Other
○ Odd	○ Sight lines	○ _____
○ Even	○ Angles	○ _____
○ Sequence	○ _____	○ _____

Home Site Matrix

Home Site #	Price	Location	Size	Shape	View	Orient.	Topo	Easemt	Limits	Number	Position	Other Considerations	Benefits/USP Advantages

Site Characteristics — Site Constraints — Cultural Considerations

Closing *(Continued)*

C8. Without a completed model

Situation

You are selling without a completed model(s) and the customer is indicating that he or she "likes" what you will have but will have to wait to see the completed models before possibly making a decision.

Strategy

Get them to admit that they like the *concept*, but that the *sole* reason they can't go ahead with the paperwork is because they *think* they need to see the completed model.

Rationale

Customers often bluff or "blow smoke." This flushes them out.

Note: Use this strategy only if your company approves of this type of contingency program.

C8. You are selling without a completed model(s) and the customer is indicating that he or she "likes" what you will have but will have to wait to see the completed models before possibly making a decision.

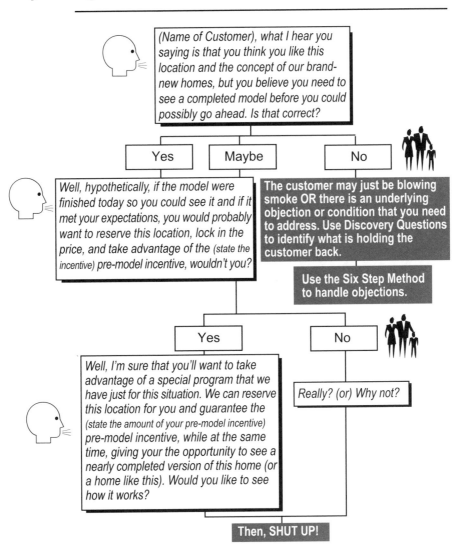

(Name of Customer), what I hear you saying is that you think you like this location and the concept of our brand-new homes, but you believe you need to see a completed model before you could possibly go ahead. Is that correct?

| Yes | Maybe | | No |

Well, hypothetically, if the model were finished today so you could see it and if it met your expectations, you would probably want to reserve this location, lock in the price, and take advantage of the (state the incentive) pre-model incentive, wouldn't you?

The customer may just be blowing smoke OR there is an underlying objection or condition that you need to address. Use Discovery Questions to identify what is holding the customer back.

Use the Six Step Method to handle objections.

| Yes | | No |

Well, I'm sure that you'll want to take advantage of a special program that we have just for this situation. We can reserve this location for you and guarantee the (state the amount of your pre-model incentive) pre-model incentive, while at the same time, giving your the opportunity to see a nearly completed version of this home (or a home like this). Would you like to see how it works?

Really? (or) Why not?

Then, SHUT UP!

Key

Customer response   Professional Communicator

NOTICE

CAUTION! This form is for concept and reference purposes only. Before using it or any variation thereof, you are advised to seek the advice of legal counsel.

CONTINGENCY ADDENDUM

PURCHASER'S OPTION TO INSPECT MODEL

This addendum to purchase agreement date _____ is by and between
_____, as Seller, and
_____, as Purchaser(s).

Anything in the foregoing Purchase Agreement to the contrary notwithstanding the following terms and conditions shall apply:

This Purchase Agreement is contingent upon and subject to Purchaser(s) having the option and right to inspect the model(s) being constructed by Seller at the Development (which may or may not be the same floor plan Purchaser(s) has selected), under the following terms:

1. Seller shall notify Purchaser(s) in writing setting forth a date after which the model(s) is sufficiently completed so as to enable Purchaser(s) to determine if it fits their needs; and

2. Purchaser(s) shall have _____ business days from the date set forth in said notice to inspect such model(s), at which time the Purchaser(s) shall have the following options:

    a. Remove the contingency set forth herein, in which event this Purchase Agreement shall be in full force and effect; and

    b. Notify the Seller in writing that the model does not meet their needs, in which case the Purchase Agreement shall become null and void and Seller shall return the earnest money deposit tendered therewith.

3. If and in the event the Purchaser(s) does not notify the Seller in writing, within the _____ period set forth, and as provided for in Paragraph 2 above, this contingency shall expire and shall have no further effect, and in that event, the terms and conditions of the Purchase Agreement shall remain in full force and effect.

As used above, "sufficiently completed" shall mean:
_____

The above terms and conditions are accepted:

WITNESSES: SELLER:
                                    (Company Name)
_____   BY: _____
_____   DATE: _____

                                    PURCHASER(S)

_____   _____
_____   _____
                                    DATE: _____

CAUTION! This form is for concept and reference purposes only. Before using it or any variation thereof, you are advised to seek the advice of legal counsel.

Closing *(Continued)*

C9. Uncovering obstacles

Situation

Customers are indicating an interest, but they present some kind of obstacle to overcome—an unresolved job transfer, a house to sell, an impending legal settlement, a divorce, or the like. The buyers are giving you "buying signals" that indicate some issue is standing in the way of making a decision.

Strategy

Get them to acknowledge the objection—verbally and emotionally—and to make a "decision" that if the condition they are talking about didn't exist, they would want to go ahead and reserve their choice homesite, lock in the price, and get the process started. When they acknowledge that, you "hypothetically" remove that obstacle and "test close" to find out if they are serious about buying, subject only to those conditions or if they are just "blowing smoke" and using the supposed obstacle as a ploy.

Find out their frame of reference as to the length of time it might take to remove or resolve this condition.

Rationale

If what the customers are posing is a legitimate obstacle and you remove it, then you can move forward.

C9. Customers are indicating an interest, but they present some kind of obstacle to overcome.

(Customers' names), it seems that you are indicating that you like this home, the area, and the homesite, and that you would like to lock in the price, but you are obviously concerned about (job transfer, selling the house, legal settlement, etc.), *correct?*

Wait for their response. Then continue with...

Hypothetically, (customers' names), if your (job transfer were secured today), **(or)** (house were sold and closed today), **(or)** (whatever obstacle were resolved today), *you probably would like to start the process to reserve this homesite and lock in the price, right?*

Pause and wait for their response. Their response will be a "decision."

No.	Yes.
The customers have just said that the condition they previously stated is NOT standing in their way. Therefore, there must be another reason. This response is now an objection, to which you would reply...	If you are in a position to offer a contingent or conditional agreement, subject to the point in time when their stated condition will be removed or resolved, continue with...

Oh really? Why not?

(Customers' names)—When do you think your (job transfer might be secured), **(or)** (house sold), **(or)** (whatever obstacle might be resolved)?

Continued on the next page.

Key
Customer response | Professional Communicator

C9. Customers are indicating an interest, but they present some kind of obstacle to overcome. *(continued)*

Continued from previous page.

If the customers give you a time frame that is outside your ability to provide a contingency, state...

With that in mind, (customers' names), may I ask you a question? Do you think you will be moving to (city) regardless of whether you transfer goes through with the company?

Wait for a response.

(Customers' names) you are saying that you are not sure when the (transfer) will be coming through. Well, it seems that you have two options open to you. You can keep looking, but anything you would see today probably won't be available.

Proceed with...

(Customers' names), I understand that you are saying you would not be prepared to go ahead because of the uncertainty of your (transfer), so I would not want you to get all excited about a home you couldn't have. However, would you consider this idea?
If you found a home that you loved, would you consider going ahead with a refundable contingency option, which would allow you, oh let's say (state the time it would take to resolve or be assured).

Wait for a response.

What you are looking for is their frame of reference. They could respond with "one, two, or three months," which would be their time frame to "fix" the condition. Wait for a response and continue with...

In order to reserve your homesite, lock the price, and to give you the comfort of having the opportunity to assure yourselves of your (job transfer), (or) (house sold), (or) (whatever obstacle resolved), we can get the paperwork started today and make it totally conditional upon your (job transfer), (or) (house selling), (or) (whatever obstacle) by (date). With that in mind, do you have any more questions before we take a look at how that would work?

At that point, you have their money and a psychological commitment. Since you will have some money as a deposit, you are assured you will meet them again.

If all else fails, use SST 22 on page 154 or SST 24 on page 158.

Key
Customer response — Professional Communicator

Closing *(Continued)*

C10. Number of NOs

Situation

Sales and, therefore, compensation will increase in direct proportion to the number of NOs that you receive from a customer during a presentation.

Strategy

Pose a question that, regardless of the customer's answer, will either elicit a positive indication of interest to go to the next step or it will raise a question or objection.

Rationale

This closing question will only elicit one of two possible answers.

▶ A question or an objection from the customer

▶ A "decision" in the form of a commitment to take the next step.

C10. Sales and, therefore, compensation will increase in direct proportion to the number of **NO**s that you receive from a customer during a presentation.

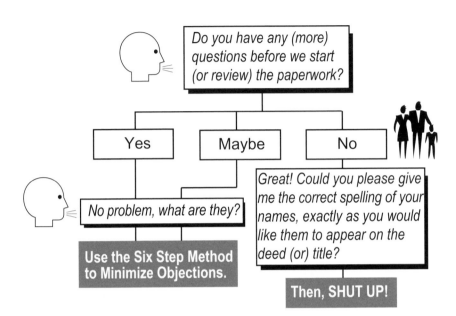

Do you have any (more) questions before we start (or review) the paperwork?

Yes   Maybe   No

No problem, what are they?

Use the Six Step Method to Minimize Objections.

Great! Could you please give me the correct spelling of your names, exactly as you would like them to appear on the deed (or) title?

Then, SHUT UP!

Key

Customer response   Professional Communicator

Closing *(Continued)*

C11. Little decisions

Situation

During the presentation and selection process, you have an opportunity to gauge the customers' level of interest, prompt them into making *little decisions*, and determine if they are ready to go to the next step.

Strategy

Ask open-ended *discovery* questions, which, depending on how they answer, could become closing questions.

Rationale

Trial closes (test closes) at any appropriate time during a presentation to get a decision are an excellent way of determining the customers' level of interest and to judge whether you are moving the customer through the process of elimination successfully.

C11. During the presentation and selection process, you have an opportunity to gauge the customers' level of interest, prompt them into making *little decisions*, and determine if they are ready to go to the next step.

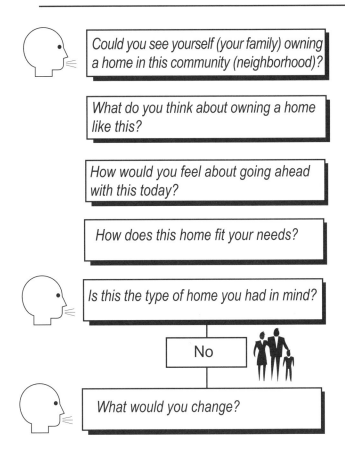

Could you see yourself (your family) owning a home in this community (neighborhood)?

What do you think about owning a home like this?

How would you feel about going ahead with this today?

How does this home fit your needs?

Is this the type of home you had in mind?

No

What would you change?

Key

Customer response

Professional Communicator

Closing *(Continued)*

C12. Feedback-oriented involvement

Situation

Throughout the presentation, you have an opportunity to present many **feedback-oriented involvement** questions.

Strategy

Gauge their level of interest and obtain "little decisions" by asking questions that offer the customers a choice of possibilities. Present at least three such questions in every presentation.

Rationale

These are sometimes known as "alternatives of choice" questions. This type of question helps to lead the customers through the process of elimination and help them visualize themselves living in the home.

C12. Throughout the presentation, you have an opportunity to present many feedback-oriented involvement questions such as the following examples.

Selections

In your new home, do you want (or) prefer oak* (or) walnut* cabinets?

*Use examples appropriate to your situation.

Options

Which would work better for you, brick* (or) stone*?

*Use examples appropriate to your situation.

Garage location

On this particular home site, do you think the garage would be best on the right or left of the home site?

Move In Date

Would you prefer to move into your new home around the 1st or the 15th of (state the month)?

Cash or Mortgage

Would it be better for the agreement to read cash or will you be obtaining financing?

Financing Plans

Would you prefer the 15-year or the 30-year financing program? (or)

Would you prefer that the agreement contain 80% or 90% financing?

Site Location

Would you prefer the corner or the cul-de-sac location? (or)

Would you prefer that we build your home on the lake or the golf course site? (or)

Would you prefer the home with the boat dock or the one close to the tennis courts?

New Home Orientation

Would a weekday or weekend be more convenient to schedule your new home orientation before moving in?

Bank-Credit Interview

Would you like me to schedule your meeting with (name of person and title) at (name of financial institution) for Wednesday, or would Thursday be best?

Exposure Location

Would you like eastern or southwestern exposure?

Key

Customer response — Professional Communicator

Closing (Continued)

C13. Small commitments

Situation

Many times during a presentation you will have the opportunity to prompt the customer to make a series of small commitments through little decisions, using the alternative of choice technique.

Strategy

Take C12 to the next level. Add an assumptive statement to the beginning of an alternative of choice feedback-oriented question using similar examples from the previous SST on page 135.

Rationale

Closing is a continuous process of elimination. Alternatives of choice enable the customer to visualize the finished home by selecting his or her own possibilities for the home. With a series of small commitments it is much easier to close.

C13. Many times during a presentation you will have the opportunity to prompt the customer to make a series of small commitments through little decisions, using the alternative of choice technique.

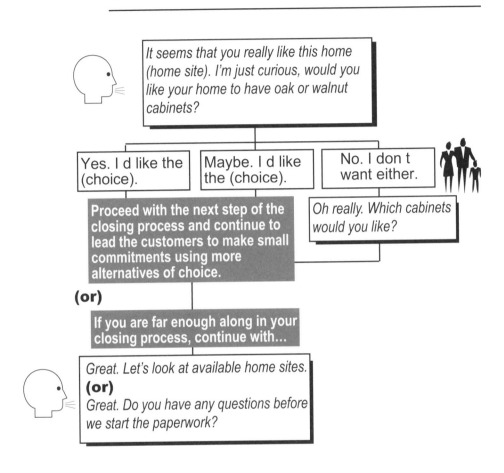

Professional Communicator: It seems that you really like this home (home site). I'm just curious, would you like your home to have oak or walnut cabinets?

Yes. I d like the (choice).

Maybe. I d like the (choice).

No. I don t want either.

Proceed with the next step of the closing process and continue to lead the customers to make small commitments using more alternatives of choice.

Oh really. Which cabinets would you like?

(or)

If you are far enough along in your closing process, continue with...

Great. Let's look at available home sites.
(or)
Great. Do you have any questions before we start the paperwork?

Key
Customer response
Professional Communicator

Closing *(Continued)*

C14. Not alone

Situation

The customer is raising objections or concerns that other now-satisfied customers have also experienced.

Strategy

Tell the customer he or she is not "alone" in this thinking. Relate an example of someone else who was in the same position as your customer is.

Rationale

The other customers had questions and were hesitant, but made the decision to go ahead and today are very happy that they did. This leads you into showing testimonials from "expert" witnesses.

C14. The customer is raising objections or concerns that other now-satisfied customers have also experienced.

> Common objection.

That's a great (good) question. In fact, all of (many of*) our home buyers have asked that exact same question.

(or**)

> Turning to a book of testimonials.

*I know you **feel** very concerned about (restate whatever the concern or question is). However, we've had other people who've had the same exact concerns. As a matter of fact, I have some letters from some of them that I'd like to show you.*

*Whichever is more appropriate.

**Really skilled professional communicators will use both options.

Closing *(Continued)*

C15. Indicated interest

Situation

Customer poses a question that indicates interest. Example: Customer says *"Do you have 90% financing?"* (-or-) *"Can I get a three-car garage?"* (-or-) *"Do you have corner home sites?"*

Strategy

Feed the question back with an inquisitive tone, so that the customers' answer is a decision that continues to confirm ownership.

Rationale

This type of closing question puts the ball back into the customer's court (selling is like tennis).

C15. Customer poses a question that indicates interest.

If you are listening carefully, there will be many opportunities in a presentation to use this technique.

Can we get 90% financing?

Oh, are you thinking about acquiring your new home with 90% financing?

Yes

Can I get a three-car garage?

Oh, is having a three-car garage important to you?

Yes

Do you have corner home sites?

Oh, would you like your new home to be built on a corner homesite?

Yes

Key

Customer response

Professional Communicator

Closing *(Continued)*

C16. Test Close

Situation

During the presentation, you have an opportunity to "Test Close" on a feature in which the customer has indicated an interest.

Strategy

"Test Close" by purposefully making an incorrect statement. This is a great strategy to use within the first few minutes of the customers' *first return* visit.

Rationale

Get to the point for their return visit instead of engaging in small talk and pleasantries. People like to correct "mistakes." This also interrupts their expectation level and causes a "knee-jerk" response to correct the mistake, which will cause them to make a decision and get to the point quickly.

C16. During the presentation, you have an opportunity to "Test Close" on a feature in which the customer has indicated an interest.

The customers previously told you or you observed or understood they liked
- Architectural style A
- Home site 7
- Oak cabinets
- etc., etc.

Now, (Name of Customer), you said you were interested in…
(Architectural style **B***)* **(or)**
Home site **10** **(or)**
the **maple** *cabinets, etc..*

The customer will probably correct you.

No, it was Architectural style A (or) the oval shaped pool (or) Home site 7 (or) the oak cabinets.

Oh, yes, of course.

Use only one "incorrect" statement close per customer.

If they agree with your "incorrect" statement, don't argue with them. Just agree and proceed forward.

Key
Customer response   Professional Communicator

Closing *(Continued)*

C17. Take it away

Situation

What the customers want is in short supply but they are indicating difficulty in making a decision. Assume they like a choice home site or a completed home that could be acquired soon by someone else.

Strategy

Create urgency through scarcity.

Rationale

Get the customers to acknowledge and decide that they don't want to risk losing it by taking it away.

C17. What the customers want is in short supply but they are indicating difficulty in making a decision.

I believe that you really like this (home or home site, etc.) with its...(restate the benefits with emotional involvement), is that right? Well, I have a suggestion that might avoid some disappointment.

As you know, this is the only (state what it is) that we have available at the moment! In the event someone else acquires (your home/home site**) before you come back, let's pick out another one, **almost as nice**.*

*(or) We only have (state number) of these (homes/home sites) available.

**(or) ...makes your home their home...

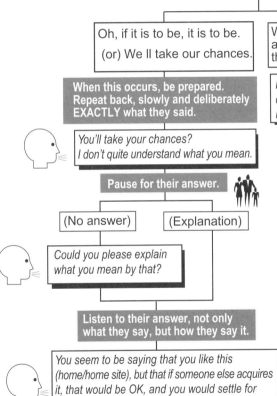

Oh, if it is to be, it is to be.

(or) We ll take our chances.

We don t want something almost as nice. We want this one.

When this occurs, be prepared. Repeat back, slowly and deliberately EXACTLY what they said.

Fine. Do you have any more questions before we start (or) review the paperwork?

You'll take your chances? I don't quite understand what you mean.

Pause for their answer.

(No answer)   (Explanation)

Could you please explain what you mean by that?

Pause for their answer.

May I make an observation? You (folks) don't seem like the "second best" people to me.

Am I right about that?

Pause for their answer.

Really though, could it possibly be a question about the affordability?

Listen to their answer, not only what they say, but how they say it.

*You seem to be saying that you like this (home/home site), but that if someone else acquires it, that would be OK, and you would settle for **second best**?*

Then proceed back to presentation or review of the financing opportunities.

See next strategy.

Key

Customer response   Professional Communicator

Closing *(Continued)*

C18. Explain the takeaway

Situation

In response to the "takeaway" close, the customer says *"Oh, come on..."* (-or-) *"Who are you kidding?"* (-or-) *"That's a little too pushy, etc."*

Strategy

Show a sincere interest in the customer, while at the same time continue finding out their true level of interest.

Rationale

People appreciate your concern if you are sincere.

C18. In response to the "takeaway" close, the customer says *"Oh, come on."*

I believe that you really like this (home or home site, etc.) with its…(restate the benefits with emotional involvement). Is that right? Well, I have a suggestion that might avoid some disappointment.

As you know, this is the only (state what it is) that we have available at the moment! In the event someone else acquires (your home/home site**) before you come back, let's pick out another one, **almost as nice**.*

*(or) We only have (state number) of these (homes/home sites) available.

**(or) …makes your home their home…

Oh, come on. (or)

Who are you kidding?

When this occurs, be prepared.

Well, in the past, people (folks) just like you have come back a few days after having made the decision that they wanted the home, and were extremely disappointed when they were told that it was no longer available for them. In fact, people sometimes actually become angry because they feel it had not been explained clearly to them what could happen. I just don't want that to occur with you (folks). I hope you understand I'm sincere about that. With that in mind, it makes good sense to go ahead today, lock in the price, and make this home your home, doesn't it?

Key

Customer response | Professional Communicator

Closing *(Continued)*

C19. Uncomfortable with closing

Situation

Customer says, *"You're being too pushy!"* (-or-) *"You're closing too hard!"* (-or-) they don't say anything, but their body language or remarks direct you to the fact that they are getting uncomfortable with your closing attempts.

Strategy

Ease the tension and transition back into the process.

NOTE: This Smart Selling™ Technique is for concept purposes. Understand the concept and then create a script that you are *comfortable with* and that you can convey with warmth and sincerity.

Rationale

People appreciate your concern if you are sincere.

C19. Customer says, "You're being too pushy!" (-or-) "You're closing too hard!" (-or-) they don't say anything.

(Name of customer), I am sorry. I sense that something is making you uncomfortable right now. Am I right?

Pause for their answer.

Please don't confuse my enthusiasm with being pushy! You know I am excited for you!

Don't pause.

My purpose, (name of customer), isn't to try and sell you a home. It isn't even to try and convince you to buy a home. You are out exploring the opportunities on your own and I understand and respect that.

But, I sincerely would like to help you find a home in our community that best fits your needs. Does that make sense? I need you to help me help you!

Smile warmly and say:

Let's change gears for a moment. I've been doing a lot of talking, now it's your turn. What are your thoughts?

Listen, take notes, then subtly go back to your presentation.

Although they shouldn't, some representatives have their favorite homes. If you haven't found out all of the customer's needs, you may appear to be pushing your choice rather than what the customer wants.

Key

Customer response — Professional Communicator

Closing *(Continued)*

C20. We don't have our checkbook with us

Situation

In the closing process, you have asked a final closing question and it appears that the customers have made a decision to go ahead but they say, **"We don't have our checkbook with us."**

Strategy

Get them to reaffirm that they want the home regardless of whether they have their checkbook with them or not and make it easy for them to move forward by taking away their defined obstacle.

Rationale

Customers sometimes bluff or blow smoke. By offering an easy solution, you now provide them with an opportunity to make a commitment, ask more questions, or raise further objections.

Also, when they give you any amount of money, they have made a commitment. Further, because you have something that belongs to them (money), you are guaranteed you will see them face-to-face again.

C20. In the closing process, you have asked a final closing question and it appears that the customers have made a decision to go ahead but they say, "We don't have our checkbook with us."

No problem. You're saying that you like this home and would be ready to go ahead and secure your home site and start the paperwork to lock in the price except for the fact that you don't have your checkbook with you now, is that correct?

Yes

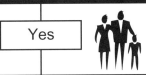

Oh, I understand. So that we can reserve your choice location, lock in the price, and make this home yours today, any denomination of cash* can get the process started. About how much do you have with you?

Then, SHUT UP!

Well, we only have ($50) cash on us.

Great, let's start the paperwork.

Write the full agreement noting "with cash balance of (balance of deposit) due on or before 5PM on (Day, Date—no more than three days later)."
If it's a busy day and you don't have time to write a full agreement,
at least get a reservation with the balance due, similarly stated on a specific day and time.

*Only use this SST if your company approves or allows you to take cash deposits.

Closing *(Continued)*

C21. Can't afford it

Situation

The customer has indicated that they love the home and want it, but are afraid they cannot afford it.

Strategy

Show a sincere interest in the customer, while at the same time continue finding out their true level of interest and closing for an appointment using the alternative of choice method.

Rationale

People appreciate your concern when you are sincere.

C21. The customer has indicated that they love the home and want it, but are afraid they cannot afford it.

As part of our total service, we have established a fine working relationship* with some of the leading financial institutions in the area who will be happy to meet with you at your convenience to reassure you and provide you with any additional information you many need to make it easy for you to own this home. I will be happy to set your appointment with (name of person at the financial institution). Would today or tomorrow (this morning/this afternoon) be better?

*Change this appropriately if your company has an in-house mortgage company or an affiliate financial organization.

Closing *(Continued)*

C22. Think it over

Situation

Customer(s) says, *"I (we) want to think it over."*

Strategy

Get the customer to think through the opportunity with you, hopefully to uncover the real objection—probably the money.

Rationale

Allow the customer to "think it over" in your presence while using the process of elimination.

NOTE: This Smart Selling Technique is for concept purposes. Understand the concept and then create a script that you are *comfortable with* and that you can convey with warmth and sincerity.

C22. Customer(s) says, "I (we) want to think it over."

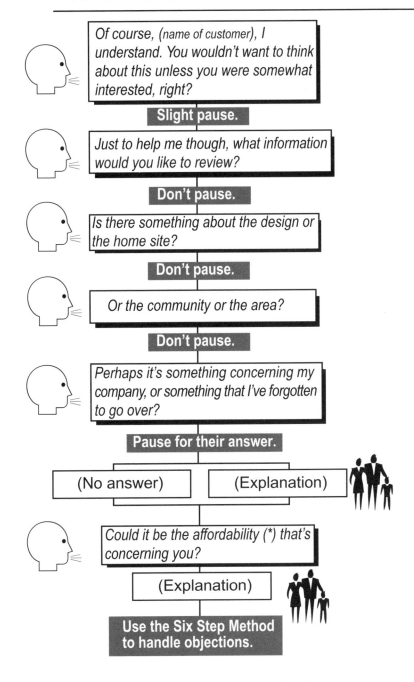

Of course, (name of customer), I understand. You wouldn't want to think about this unless you were somewhat interested, right?

Slight pause.

Just to help me though, what information would you like to review?

Don't pause.

Is there something about the design or the home site?

Don't pause.

Or the community or the area?

Don't pause.

Perhaps it's something concerning my company, or something that I've forgotten to go over?

Pause for their answer.

(No answer)   (Explanation)

Could it be the affordability (*) that's concerning you?

(Explanation)

Use the Six Step Method to handle objections.

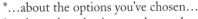

*…about the options you've chosen…
*…about the selections you've made…
*…about home site #75…
*…about the total package…

Key
Customer response   Professional Communicator

Closing *(Continued)*

C23. Easy answer

Situation

After you ask a final closing question and receive a positive response or no negative feedback, ask a question to which the answer can be given easily without thinking.

Strategy

Make a smooth transition into starting the purchase agreement.

NOTE: This Smart Selling Technique is for concept purposes. Understand the concept and then create a script that you are *comfortable with* and that you can convey with warmth and sincerity.

Rationale

This type of close guides the customer to continue to express their feelings openly.

C23. After you ask a final closing question and receive a positive response or no negative feedback, ask a question to which the answer can be given easily without thinking.

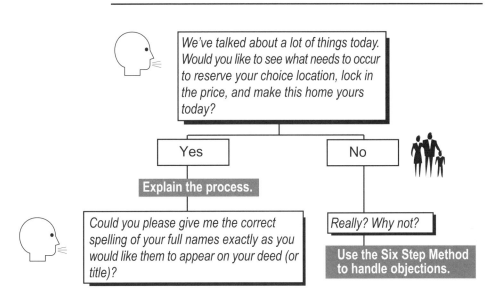

We've talked about a lot of things today. Would you like to see what needs to occur to reserve your choice location, lock in the price, and make this home yours today?

Yes

No

Explain the process.

Could you please give me the correct spelling of your full names exactly as you would like them to appear on your deed (or title)?

Really? Why not?

Use the Six Step Method to handle objections.

Key

Customer response

Professional Communicator

Closing *(Continued)*

C24. Not the real objection

Situation

When it seems that nothing else will work and the customer will not give you the real objection.

Strategy

Take the customer through the thought process at the "perceived" end of the presentation and find out the "real" or "hidden" objection.

NOTE: This Smart Selling Technique is for concept purpose. Understand the concept and then create a script that you are *comfortable with* and that you can convey with warmth and sincerity.

Rationale

Summarizing the benefits, ask the customers where you've "failed." Of course, you probably haven't "failed," and they will tell you so. Therefore, the customers will be prompted to give you the real objection. People will appreciate your concern if you are sincere.

C24. When it seems that nothing else will work and the customer will not give you the real objection.

(Name of customers), *before you leave, can I ask you one more question that may help me in the future?*

Pause.

So that I don't make the same mistake again with another customer, will you please tell me, what I did wrong?

Pause.

Oh, nothing. You were great. You did nothing wrong, etc.

Well, I appreciate that, but obviously I didn't help you experience the real value of this home and community because based on all the things you've told me and all the features and benefits we've discussed as being important to you, this home seems ideal!

Don't pause. With sincerity say...

Of course, this is a big decision for you. What are your concerns about making this home yours?

Listen carefully. Use the Six Step Method to handle objections.

Key
Customer response — Professional Communicator

Closing *(Continued)*

C25. Hidden fears

Situation

The customers appear to be having a hard time making a commitment because of a subconscious fear of the "risk(s)" they perceive may be involved in taking the next step forward.

Strategy

Identify the possible reasons for the customers' fears (to name and isolate the fears) and justify the benefits of making the commitment to move forward.

Use a logical four-step process that—with customer involvement—will cause the customer to experience the advantages of discovering how to manage "risk," and the possible downside of simply avoiding it.

Rationale

This is achieved through a logical four-step process that—with customer involvement—will cause the customer to experience the advantages of discovering how to manage "risk," and the possible downside of simply avoiding it.

By taking customers through a very logical pro/con, +/- analysis, they will conclude on their own what is best.

NOTE: This closing strategy is based on a "Risk Analysis" Technique created and taught by noted speaker, author, and consultant Nido Qubein.

C25. The customers appear to be having a hard time making a commitment because of a subconscious fear of the "risk(s)" they perceive may be involved in taking the next step forward.

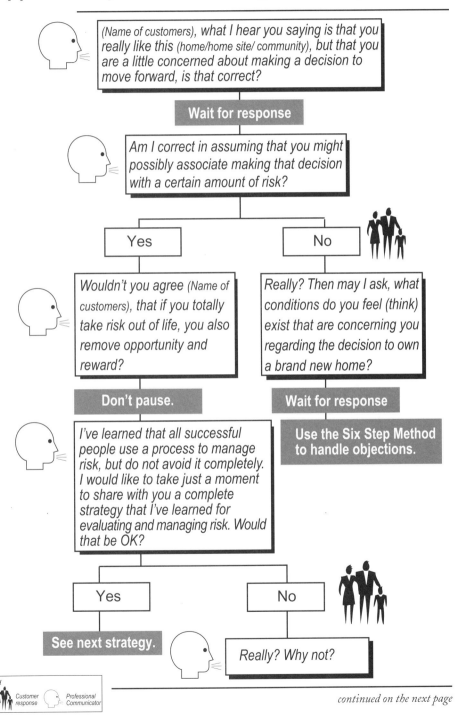

(Name of customers), what I hear you saying is that you really like this (home/home site/ community), but that you are a little concerned about making a decision to move forward, is that correct?

Wait for response

Am I correct in assuming that you might possibly associate making that decision with a certain amount of risk?

Yes

Wouldn't you agree (Name of customers), that if you totally take risk out of life, you also remove opportunity and reward?

Don't pause.

I've learned that all successful people use a process to manage risk, but do not avoid it completely. I would like to take just a moment to share with you a complete strategy that I've learned for evaluating and managing risk. Would that be OK?

Yes

See next strategy.

No

Really? Why not?

No

Really? Then may I ask, what conditions do you feel (think) exist that are concerning you regarding the decision to own a brand new home?

Wait for response

Use the Six Step Method to handle objections.

Key
Customer response
Professional Communicator

continued on the next page

C25. The customers appear to be having a hard time making a commitment because of a subconscious fear of the "risk(s)."
(continued)

---

1. Take out a *Managing Decisions—Minimizing Risk Customer Worksheet* **(on page 167).**
2. Ask them about any perceived benefits to owning a new home.
3. Refer to your study sheet to relate benefits to customer "Hot Buttons."

1. Space	3. Lifestyle	5. Something New
2. Location	4. Status (Ego)	6. Financial Advantage or Opportunity

What are some of the benefits that you would enjoy as a result of owning this brand new home that you would like to add?

**Pause and wait for response.
Put anything they say on the list.**

OK. Do you have any questions or comments so far?

Wait for response

The second step in the process is to explore the possibilities of any "worst things" that could happen as a result of owning this brand new home (site). What are any bad things that you could think might happen?

4. **Write in any perceived conditions they may mention on the**
Managing Decisions—Minimizing Risk Customer Worksheet.

If they come up with any conditions, proceed with...	If they cannot come up with any conditions, proceed with...

The third step is to explore what could be done to minimize or overcome the possible "worst things that could happen."

See next strategy.

Well then, congratulations. There doesn't appear to be any reason(s) whatsoever for you not to take advantage of all the positive benefits, does there? So that we can reserve this location and lock in the price, do you have any questions before we start the paperwork?

Key

Customer response — Professional Communicator

continued on the next page

C25. The customers appear to be having a hard time making a commitment because of a subconscious fear of the "risk(s)."

(continued)

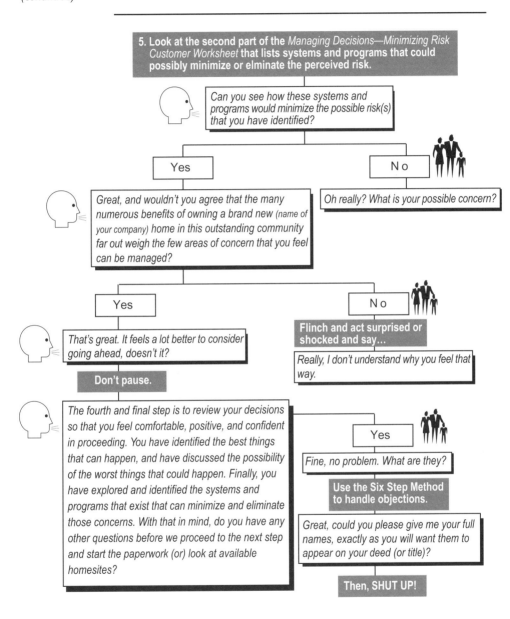

Managing Decisions—Minimizing Risk
Customer Worksheet

Benefits of Owning   **Perceived "Worst That Could Happen"**

+   –

_____   _____

_____   _____

_____   _____

_____   _____

Systems or programs that could possibly minimize or eliminate the perceived risks.

- ❏ Pre-qualification
  (Homesite/Financing Contingency)
- ❏ Incentives Program
- ❏ Pre-Close Walk-Through
  (New Home Orientation)
- ❏ Testimonials
- ❏ Copies of Warranties
- ❏ New Homes Vs. Used Homes Benefits
- ❏ Down Payment Options
- ❏ Insurance
- ❏ Move-In Checklist
- ❏ Builder Buy Back Satisfaction Guarantee*
- ❏ School District Report Card
- ❏ Church Invitations
- ❏ Move-In Gift Baskets
- ❏ Move-In Survival Kit
- ❏

- ❏ Return of Earnest Money Guarantee
- ❏ Home Owners' Guide
- ❏ Home Owner Orientation
- ❏ References
- ❏ Technical Data
- ❏ Comparison of Renting Vs. Buying
- ❏ Mortgage Program Options
- ❏ Refinancing Options
- ❏ Mortgage Protection Programs
- ❏ Utility Bill Comparisons
- ❏ Moving Guide and Assistance Program
- ❏ New Resident Information
- ❏ Vendor Coupons
- ❏
- ❏

*(if applicable)

Managing Decisions—Minimizing Risk
Representative Study Sheet

"Best That Could Happen"

Benefits to convey related to these "Hot Buttons."

1. More Space or Less Space
2. To Change Location
   - Benefits of location
   - Schools
3. Lifestyle
   - Improved or enhanced lifestyle
   - Benefits of amenities
   - Stability/Security
   - Peace of mind
4. Status or Ego
   - Pride of ownership
   - Uniqueness
   - Technology
5. To Have Something "New"
   - Utility bill savings
   - Building Equity
   - Customization or Personalization
   - Warranty
   - Technology
6. Financial Advantage or Opportunity
   - Tax savings
   - Investment
   - Appreciation
   - Incentives*
   - Closing costs paid*

(*if applicable)

Note: These are generic examples. Study each column and identify benefits and solutions/systems/resources that are appropriate and applicable to your situation.

"Worst That Could Happen"

Systems or programs that could possibly minimize risk and eliminate the fear of...

1. Change
2. Doing Business with a Builder
   - Return of earnest money guarantee
   - Builder buy back satisfaction guarantee*
   - Pre-close walk-through
   - Testimonials
   - Copies of warranties
   - New homes vs. used homes benefits
3. The Unknown
   - New resident information
   - Vendor coupons
   - Testimonials
   - School district report card
   - Church invitations
4. Moving
   - Moving guide and assistance program
   - Move-in checklist
   - New resident information
   - Vendor coupons
   - Testimonials
   - Church invitations
   - Move-in gift baskets
   - Move-in survival kit
5. The Financial Process
   - Mortgage payment options
   - Refinancing options
   - Mortgage protection programs
   - Pre-qualification
   - Builder buy back satisfaction guarantee*
   - Down payment options
6. Financial Obligation
   - Comparison of renting vs. buying
   - Refinancing options
   - Mortgage protection programs
   - Utility bill comparisons
   - Builder buy back satisfaction guarantee*
   - Incentives program
   - Down payment options

Closing *(Continued)*

C26. After the paperwork

Situation

After completing the paperwork.

Strategy

Ease into the approval of the paperwork and remove the feeling and sense of "finality" that accompanies this part of the selling process.

Rationale

This type of close continues the dialogue (like a volley in tennis) and allows the customers to make a little decision about a future event. It makes the customers more comfortable about making the "big" decision.

C26. After completing the paperwork.

> *Congratulations on taking the first step! With your approval right here, we'll begin the process. This allows us to secure your home (home site), lock in the price, and enables us to proceed forward with your (state something like...) loan approval* **(or)** *carpet and tile installation* **(or)** *preparing your home for you to move into it, etc.*

Closing *(Continued)*

C27. Buyer's remorse

Situation

After the customer has concluded the initial paperwork and to prepare them for *"buyer's remorse."*

Strategy

Establish an expectation level and to let them know that *"buyer's remorse"* is normal.

NOTE: Present this just before they leave, and almost as an *"afterthought,"* with warmth, sincerity, and a good-natured sense of humor, just like "Columbo."

Rationale

It is easier for them to deal with the unknown when you show them that's not a big deal.

C27. After the customer has concluded the initial paperwork and to prepare them for *"buyer's remorse."*

Oh, just one more thing…it is not uncommon that sometime after you leave today, you might think—or someone might say to you—"Why are you buying a new home?"

If that happens, it's perfectly OK and it happens to almost everyone.

It's called "buyer's remorse" and it's quite normal.

Then take two jellybeans (or other candy) from a jar on your desk. While smiling, and with a slight chuckle, proceed with...

These are buyer's remorse pills. If it should happen, remember, it's OK. Just take one of these and call me in the morning, OK?

Key
Customer response
Professional Communicator

We're Looking for Success!

Have A Great Sales Technique?

Want To Have It Included In Our Next Book?

In our continual pursuit of excellence and to constantly keep new home sales professionals on the *"cutting edge,"* we are always creating new training materials and publishing books.

If you think you have a new home sales strategy or technique that is exceptional, and would like to have it considered for possible inclusion, send it to:

New Home Specialist^{SM} Education Systems
2300 Glades Road
Suite 400 West
Boca Raton, Florida 33431
Phone: (561) 368-1151
Fax: (561) 368-1171
E-mail: info@newhomespecialist.com
Website: www.newhomespecialist.com

New Home Specialist[SM] Publishing Group

Join other new homes sales professionals who are benefiting from The Official New Home Sales Development System®.

	Qty	Unit Price	Total
The Official Handbook for New Home Salespeople by Bob Schultz		$34.95[1]	$
Smart Selling[SM] Techniques by Bob Schultz		$34.95[1]	$
Selling to Multicultural Home Buyers: The Official Guide for New Home Salespeople by Michael D. Lee		$34.95[1]	$
The Five Minute Professional—A 9-Tape Audio Cassette System by Bob Schultz		$125.00[1]	$
Smart Start[SM] by Marilyn McVay		$99.95[2]	$
The Official New Home Sales Development System® Video, Volume I by Bob Schultz		$1,495.00[3]	$
The Official System for New Home Sales Follow-Through® by Steve Hoffacker		$695.00[4]	$
The Official System for New Home Sales Consumer Research[SM] by Steve Hoffacker		$695.00[4]	$
♦ *You Can't Manage What You Don't Measure[SM]* Management System Reports (Computer Diskettes in Excel '97 Format) *Sales Performance Analysis* - Measure the Effectiveness of Each Salesperson		$99.95[1]	$
♦ *Marketing & Sales Cost Efficiency Analysis*—Measure the Effectiveness of Your Marketing Dollars		$99.95[1]	$
♦ *SPECIAL!* BOTH SYSTEMS FOR JUST...		$159.95[1]	$

TOTAL OF ITEMS ORDERED	$
FL Residents, please add 6% sales tax	$
[1]Shipping & Handling: $6.95 for first item; $3.75 for each add'l item	$
[2]Shipping & Handling: $9.95 for first item; $5.00 for each add'l item	$
[3]Shipping & Handling: $14.50 for each Video System	$
[4]Shipping & Handling: $12.95 for first item; $7.00 for each add'l item	$
All shipping via UPS Groundtrack. For International or FedEx, please call for shipping charges.	$
TOTAL	$

Prices subject to change without prior notification.

Complete reverse side with Personal Ordering Information

To Fax Your Order: (561) 368-1171.

For Phone Orders Or Customer Service: (561) 368-1151.

Personal Ordering Information

METHOD OF PAYMENT (US Funds Only)

❑ Enclosed check for TOTAL made payable to New Home Specialist Inc.

❑ Please charge TOTAL to my American Express/Visa/MasterCard:

(Please circle one)

Account #_____

Expiration Date: _____

Signature: _____

(Required for all charge orders)

Date: _____

Name: _____

Company: _____

Address: _____

City: _____

State:_____ Zip: _____

Phone: (   ) _____   Fax: (   ) _____

E-mail _____

Are your sales represented by: ❑ Realtor   ❑ In-House Staff
                                ❑ No. of Sales Associates _____   No. of Communities _____

Quantity discounts are available. Call for details or to discuss the following:
❑ Sales Seminars
❑ Strategic/Tactical Planning Retreats
❑ Adaptive Selling/Adaptive Management Reports
❑ Convention programs
❑ Comprehensive Sales/Management Consulting
❑ I'd like to receive -AT NO COST- your newsletter
❑ Public Seminars, Smart Selling^{SM}, and Smart Management Seminars featuring
   BOB SCHULTZ

New Home Specialist^{SM} Education Systems

2300 Glades Road ◆ Suite 400 W ◆ Boca Raton, Florida 33431
Phone: (561) 368-1151 ◆ Fax: (561) 368-1171
Email: info@newhomespecialist.com ◆ Website: www.newhomespecialist.com

Notes

Notes

Notes

Notes

Notes

Notes